If Your Relationship Is Worth Fighting For, This Book Is For You.

We believe many relationships can be for keeps. And in this book we map out tangible, practical, *do-able* techniques for repairing a relationship, or winning back a straying partner. This can be done far more easily and scientifically and surely than you might suspect.

As students of relationships between the sexes, we have observed and analyzed our own marriages, as well as over one hundred others. The following is our prescription for making a relationship healthy again, for winning back the one you love. We think the likelihood of your being successful is far greater than you think. In fact, we're sure of it.

—Eric Weber and Steven S. Simring, M.D.

How to Win Back The One You Love

"This action-oriented handbook is chock-full of extended examples and well-taken suggestions that may just make the difference in the lives of many troubled couples."

—*Booklist*

How to
Win Back
the One
You Love

Eric Weber &
Steven S. Simring, M.D.

BANTAM BOOKS
TORONTO · NEW YORK · LONDON · SYDNEY · AUCKLAND

HOW TO WIN BACK THE ONE YOU LOVE
*A Bantam Book / published by arrangement with
Macmillan Publishing Co., Inc.*

PRINTING HISTORY
Macmillan edition published May 1983

Serialized in Complete Woman *magazine*, National Enquirer
and New Woman *magazine*.

Bantam edition / August 1984

*Bantam Books are published by Bantam Books, Inc. Its
trademark, consisting of the words "Bantam Books" and
the portrayal of a rooster, is Registered in U.S. Patent and
Trademark Office and in other countries. Marca
Registrada. Bantam Books, Inc., 666 Fifth Avenue, New
York, New York 10103.*

H 0 9 8 7 6 5 4 3 2 1

To Elmer Lee Klavans

Du wieder nun in meinen Armen!
O Dank dir, Gott, für diese Lust!
Mein Mann an meiner Brust!

O Gott, wie gross ist dein Erbarmen!
O Dank dir, Gott, für diese Lust!
Mein Weib an meiner Brust!

You again in my arms!
I thank Thee, God, for this joy!
My husband on my breast!

O God, how great is Thy mercy!
I thank Thee, God, for this joy!
My wife on my breast!

Ludwig van Beethoven
Fidelio, Act II

Contents

1   Introduction

In 1955 about one in every four American marriages ended in divorce. By 1970 a third of all married couples were breaking up before death did them part. By 1976 we reached a plateau. Statistics of the last four years indicate that for every marriage that works, another one fails.

Among our moral leaders and social scientists there is a great sense of dismay over this increasing inability of husbands and wives to live together for more than a few years at a time. Magazine articles regale us with anecdotes and figures that show how quickly and blithely Americans have learned to switch partners.

What troubles us about much that we read and hear about divorce is its hand-wringing, carping quality. One senses almost a touch of envy, the grim, Calvinist ant complaining about the grasshopper's having too much fun. On an unstated level, this aura of prohibition makes divorce sound like fun. An image comes to mind of a clergyman somewhere in the Midwest admonishing his flock *not* to behave like all those narcissistic hedonists out there in California who trade in their spouses as cavalierly as they do cars. The parishioners cluck disapprovingly. But what is the hidden message? Divorced people have more fun. True, it may be immoral to get rid of one's stale, aging mate. But having accomplished that, one gets a chance to start over, to do things right this time, to sleep with livelier, more attractive partners, to have *fun*.

We too are troubled by the growing number of divorces. But unlike our friends in the pulpit, it is not Sodom and Gomorrah that we fear. No, our concern is with an aspect of divorce that is rarely aired but desperately needs to be. We worry about the millions of people who are falling silently between the cracks of our national divorce epidemic, the people who *don't* want to be divorced, the people who are *unable* to quickly, happily, and easily find someone new. Our concern is for that growing disenfranchised army of men who suddenly appear a shadow of their former selves because their wives have deserted home and hearth to pursue a dream of self-discovery and rebirth, and for that enormous battalion of women who descend into depression because they cannot bear the prospect of living alone without the men who sat across from them at breakfast every morning for the last twenty-five years.

Implicit in much of the doomsaying over divorce is what we perceive to be a subtle but perversely misleading attitude about the state of love between men and women in America today: that it is sublimely easy for people immediately to start up with someone new. One hears the expression "playing musical chairs" in connection with serial relationships or marriages, yet there is almost no discussion of the people who are left without a chair. What about them? What about all of those forlorn souls who don't want to start up with someone new or, even more tragically, *cannot* or *do not* feel they can ever find another partner to love them.

During the last fifteen years, as observers of relations between the sexes, both of us have independently concluded that at the center of America's divorce mania is a growing number of people who are falling out of the game. With increasing frequency we encounter men and women, many of them surprisingly young and attractive, who have not reconnected, who have not found someone new and exciting out in Palm Springs or up in Newburyport with whom to start one of those marvelously rambling extended families one frequently sees these days on the covers of national news-magazines.

They are men like Arthur S., a reasonably successful suburban accountant whose wife left him and their three children two years ago to open up a crafts shop in the Bahamas. Arthur has dated only rarely since Carol went. He complains that women don't seem to be turned on by him anymore; he gets the feeling he is projecting the unmistakable aura of a loser. Arthur S. claims he still wakes up in the middle of the night near tears, missing his former wife terribly, the sense of loss even more intense than it was right after their breakup. At that time he was still under the illusion he might soon find someone new, was even excited at the prospect. Now he feels pessimistic, as if that will never happen. The divorce has also affected Arthur S.'s career and children. He cannot seem to concentrate on his practice as he once did, and his number of clients has declined dramatically. His twelve-year-old daughter, formerly an excellent student, has begun falling behind in school; and his eldest child, a seventeen-year-old son, has been brought home by the town police several times for fighting and loitering.

Elizabeth L. is the young mother of a two-year-old son. Her husband moved out of their rural community in New England several months ago to cohabit with a college student he'd met at a teachers' convention. Elizabeth L. feels bereft. Her weight has dropped fifteen pounds, and she has seen the return of the asthma symptoms she'd had as a child. She is a pretty woman with light brown eyes and a warm, accepting face, and men occasionally phone her for dates. But she refuses all of them. She has confided to us that her sexual desire has all but disappeared. She only wants her husband back.

Are these just two isolated cases, examples of pathetic characters who have not been able to snap back? Are they maladjusted, rigid, out of step with our freewheeling, liberated times? We think not. One only has to run down one's own list of relatives, acquaintances, and friends to discover at least half a dozen lonely, dismal victims of divorce. Many of those who have remained alone for a year or two never really find a lasting relationship again. And even for those who do remarry, the prognosis is not good. Statistics show that second marriages are even more likely to split up than first ones.

Recent research has made it increasingly obvious that divorce is a grossly traumatic—indeed, catastrophic—event in the lives of both parents and children. Let us briefly consider the work of two distinguished research teams that have carried out some of the first intensive studies on the effects of divorce.

Hetherington, Cox, and Cox closely followed forty-eight divorced families over two years. In an article in the October 1976 issue of *The Family Coordinator*, a professional journal, these investigators state: "At one year after divorce, which seemed to be the most stressful period for both parents, 29 of the fathers and 35 of the mothers reported that they thought the divorce might have been a mistake, that they should have tried harder to resolve their conflicts and that the alternative life styles available to them were not satisfying." That's twenty-nine out of forty-eight men and thirty-five out of forty-eight women! These numbers fell over the next year, but Hetherington and her colleagues still concluded: "Some readers may object to the term crisis used to describe the divorce experience. However, in the families we studied there were none in which at least one family member did not report distress or exhibit disrupted behavior, particularly during the first year following divorce. We did not encounter a victimless divorce."

The same research team unearthed other disturbing consequences of marital disruption.

Divorced males particularly seemed to show a peak of sexual activity and a pattern of dating a variety of women in the first year following divorce. However, the stereotyped image of the happy swinging single life was not altogether accurate. . . . Many males but few females were pleased at the increased opportunity for sexual experiences with a variety of partners immediately following divorce. However, by the end of the first year both divorced men and women were expressing a want for intimacy and a lack of satisfaction in casual sexual encounters. Women expressed particularly intense feelings about frequent casual sexual encounters, often talking of feelings of desperation, overwhelming depression, and low self-esteem following such exchanges.

Wallerstein and Kelly, another set of prominent investigators, carried out a large-scale series of longitudinal studies, where they followed families in northern California over the last decade. They too found that divorce is a highly stressful event that produces behavioral difficulties or psychological problems in anywhere between one-third and one-half of the children they studied. They point out that children of different ages cope with divorce in different ways—all badly. Preschoolers try to pretend it isn't happening or assume, no matter how carefully you explain to the contrary, that they were responsible for causing the breakup. Seven- and eight-year-olds feel a pervasive sadness, and older kids experience shame and anger.

Dr. Wallerstein was featured in an April 13, 1982, article in the science section of *The New York Times* by Maya Pines, who reported the doctor's views:

After ten years, the parents are not fighting any more. But in many cases, the children are still suffering. Some of their emotional problems are obvious, others lurk like buried land mines. In addition to the normal tasks of growing up, these children must deal with deep anger against one or both parents, with guilt, with feelings of rejection, concern about being unloved and perhaps unlovable, and a tremendous fear that they may end up with broken marriages of their own.

Other recent studies have shown the astonishing health effects of being widowed or divorced. You can't do much about the former, but the latter is a preventable disease. In his book *The Broken Heart: The Medical Consequences of Loneliness,* Dr. James Lynch provides some impressive epidemiological evidence to demonstrate that separation by death or decree is associated with a wide variety of illnesses, from heart disease to cancer.

Lynch refers to the famous Hammond report on smoking and health. He quotes Dr. Harold Morowitz of Yale University, who analyzed the statistics on premature death. To no one's surprise, smoking decreases life span . . . but so does divorce. In fact, a divorced nonsmoker has almost the same chance of dying prematurely as a married man who smokes more than twenty cigarettes per day—both approximately twice that of a nonsmoking married man.

Dr. Morowitz points out that "being divorced and a nonsmoker is slightly less dangerous than smoking a pack or more a day and staying married," and then adds, perhaps a bit flippantly, "if a man's marriage is driving him to heavy smoking, he has a delicate statistical decision to make." From his health's point of view, a man might do as well to remain married to his wife and his ciggies than to give up both.

One must now raise the question: If divorce can be so painful and destructive, why are there so many of them? Why don't we find the whole process more shocking, more darkly disturbing, more frightening? At a party one is casually informed, "Oh, guess who's getting divorced? The Harrisons. That's the third couple on Anderson Avenue this month." And, then, instead of drawing back in horror or sympathy, the guests launch into a titillated discussion of who will get the kids, the Seville, the house, the springer spaniel. But what about Mr. and Mrs. Harrison? Have things really gotten that bad between them? Do they really want to go through with the ripping asunder of a relationship that has lasted a dozen years and produced a homestead, several children, scores of pleasant memories and shared experiences, and an emotional support system that may be vastly more important to them than either has anticipated?

We wonder. We have a vague sense of unease, a suspicion that something about our popular literature and films and television shows has subtly but clearly glamorized divorce, made it seem like not such a bad alternative to boredom and sameness. Why, divorce has come to look almost, sort of, dare we say it . . . fun! An adventure.

Oh, sure, there may be a short period of confusion and grief following the breakup. Being home alone on New Year's Eve. Wondering how to start dating again. Not having one's mate around for little Amy's birthday. But that passes soon enough, and then the romance and socializing begin. Well, don't they?

Of course they do. Look at Jill Clayburgh in *An Unmarried Woman*. She finds rugged, masculine Alan Bates. And Burt Reynolds in *Starting Over*. He starts over with lovely Jill Clayburgh. Hey, wait a second—didn't she wind up with Alan Bates? No matter, divorce up on the silver screen appears to be an adventure, momentarily discombobulating but then, after that, sexy and amusing and finally . . . somehow . . . it turns into marriage again, not unlike the way Snowball metamorphosed into a two-legged man in George Orwell's *Animal Farm*.

So what's the moral? Why, get divorced and you'll have a little fun; then, when you're ready, you'll find someone even better than the one you left, someone maybe even as good-looking and as entertaining as a movie star. On top of all this, we have books like *Creative Divorce* and *The Second Time Around*, which,

at least implicitly, further advance a sense of promise
about the divorced life. In Los Angeles there is even a
Divorce Hot Line, which publicizes its number over
the airwaves. People are invited to call in and get help
in speeding up their divorce. (We wonder if there's a hot
line to help couples avoid having to use the Divorce
Hot Line.) Goodness, what are any of us staying
married for? Somewhere out there a wonderful, attractive, companionable new partner is waiting for us
with open arms. No?

Nonsense! Utter, destructive, false, and corrosive
nonsense. And yet we have come to believe it, if not
totally, at least with part of our being, particularly our
libido. Think about it. Divorce. What do you see?
Misery? Forlorn children? A hapless home at holiday
time? An empty bed when you are desperate to be
hugged and cuddled? Perhaps. But only distantly.
What clicks most sharply into mind are visions of
aquamarine swimming pools, white Club Med beaches,
glittering parties and glamorous friends, dancing cheek
to cheek in a state of blissful arousal with a new,
exciting partner. Deep down people may know better,
realize the folly of such fantasies. But do they really?

It is our contention that it is the glamorization of
divorce that has helped make it so prevalent, so easy.
And even more disturbing, it is the blind hope that
things can work out better that persuades so many
people whose gut instincts are telling them *not* to give
in, *not* to agree to divorce, *not* to finally accede to their
mate's request for freedom.

In short, divorce has become so commonplace, so
popular, so *normal,* that it is now almost old-fashioned,
non-U, to resist it. "She won't give him a divorce,"
people sneer. "What's the matter with her?"

We submit that nothing is the matter with her. It is
our belief that those who are sufficiently self-interested
to resist divorce are often far saner and more visionary
than those who would reluctantly but silently go along
with it. It seems to us that far too many people faced
with a deteriorating relationship give up too easily.

They don't want to create a scene. They don't want to exhibit their need. They don't want to crowd their mate's "space." They have foolishly swallowed the facile propaganda of the day. They don't feel free to heed their own atavistic, self-protective, internal wail that they are about to go along with something that's going to clobber the hell out of them.

We don't want that to happen. Our advice is that if you have any misgivings at all about agreeing to a separation or a divorce or anything else that seems to be signaling the end of your marriage, then you'd do well to pay careful attention to these misgivings. We think that a surprisingly large number of wounded and broken relationships are worth saving. And it is the purpose of this book to persuade those millions of men and women who are timidly wondering whether or not to fight for their straying mate that their instincts are sound. In most cases, their relationship is indeed well worth fighting for.

We would like to convince the audience for this book that there is no special grace that accrues to those who submissively permit themselves to be left. It does not ennoble you to let your mate walk out on you without putting up a struggle. And even if it did, so what? This is *your* life you're living, not someone else's in a soap opera. We have far fewer second chances than we might think in the seventy or so years we have here on earth. Thus, if you feel hurt that your mate is threatening to leave, desolate because he or she is walking out, if your instinct is to scream, "Stop! Don't leave me. I love you. I *insist* you stay!" well, then, scream it. Loudly and clearly.

Certainly, some crumbling relationships aren't worth keeping together for one extra minute. But just as certainly, far too many of the ones that fly apart could have remained functioning and productive had husbands or wives made some kind of effort to keep them together. Often all it takes to ride out a marital storm is simply to state one's intention to keep the relationship whole, no matter what is required.

You should also know that many couples we interviewed reported that, having endured a difficult time in
their relationship, they now find that they are happier
together, more at peace, more confident and at ease in
the knowledge that they need and love each other, that
now "it's for keeps."

We believe many relationships can be for keeps. And
in the following chapters we map out tangible, practical, *do-able* techniques for repairing a relationship or, if
it has already been ruptured, for winning back the
straying partner. This can be done far more easily and
scientifically and surely than you might suspect. And it
makes much greater sense to pursue such a path than
many of your friends and relatives would have you
believe.

As students of relationships between the sexes, we
have observed and analyzed our own marriages, as
well as over one hundred others. And the following is
our prescription for making a relationship healthy
again, for winning back your love. Good luck. We think
that the likelihood of your being successful in this
pursuit is far greater than you think. In fact, we're sure
of it.

2 Make Conversation, Not Love

Nothing brings a husband and wife closer than good sex. Yet nothing is harder to come by when husband and wife are not communicating. And nothing is more pathetic and misguided than the person who *initiates* lovemaking in an attempt to warm up an alienated mate, or who *accedes* to lovemaking in the belief that the alienated partner will no longer be so hostile or silent. We human beings are strange creatures. Stray dogs can achieve ecstasy within seconds after first meeting. People sometimes have to spend decades together, exchanging words and touches and glances that are "just right."

But this book is not primarily concerned with helping you and your mate experience exquisite sex, although if that is an outgrowth of it, hallelujah! Its immediate goal is to help you keep your marriage together and functioning. And the one notion that you must grasp above all others is that in most cases *talk* between you and your mate should come before anything else. In a marriage, there can hardly be such a thing as too much talk.

The problem, of course, is that in almost all crumbling relationships deep, meaningful conversation is difficult to come by. One mate feels slighted, annoyed, bored, or disgusted with the other but doesn't feel free to discuss those feelings. Instead, he or she retreats inward or begins to look for satisfaction and solace outside the marriage. This is compounded when his or her mate, sensing coolness, chooses to avoid an airing of the problem because to do so might invite criticism, anger, a fight, unpleasantness. Thus, the silence grows deeper, the problem graver. Witness the following case.

Jim, a young lawyer for a large, metropolitan law firm, comes home late for dinner. He seems in a sour, uncommunicative mood. His wife, Ellen, meets him at the door. She is tired and depressed. Her face and clothing reflect her mood. She wears no makeup, her hair hangs limp and uncombed, and her dress is drab and shapeless. Under her pretty blue eyes are dark circles. The irises themselves mirror fatigue, depression, a sense of inferiority and inadequacy. And no wonder.

Three months ago Sean was born. He is the young couple's first child. Ellen feels as if her wings have been clipped, although she does not like to admit this to herself. Up until her sixth month of pregnancy, she worked as a salesperson in a fashionable art gallery. With two salaries and no children, she and Jim were able to live extremely well. Ellen bought fashionable clothes for her size six figure, and she and Jim ate dinner out almost every night. Then the baby arrived.

Sean has been a normal, healthy child in every respect. He nurses well, naps soundly, plays happily. Yet he still takes up most of Ellen's time. In fact, she often wonders how someone so small can demand so much of her energy and her concentration. Perhaps her constant fatigue exacerbates these feelings. Sean gets up twice during the middle of the night for feedings, then wakes up to begin his day at six-thirty. Jim rarely helps out because he and Ellen have agreed that he needs all his energy for his job. Right now that is the source of 100 percent of their income.

Thus, the first three months of Ellen's motherhood have not been as delicious and fulfilling as she'd fantasized they'd be when she was pregnant. Her figure has still not returned to anywhere near its former svelteness, she hardly gets out to shop or visit with friends, and most of her companionship is supplied by Sean, who neither talks nor paints nor shows any interest in politics yet. It is easy to understand why, when Jim arrives home from the office, there is a hint of desperation about her.

It is also fairly easy to guess what Jim's reaction might be upon seeing his wife at the door. Although it would be wonderful if the human animal could be noble and kind and sympathetic and loving to those who are most needy, the sad truth is we often have the opposite reaction. When a person seems to need us more than we need him or her, we usually feel an impulse to flee. Jim doesn't feel free, of course, to express to Ellen this desire to flee. It would be too cruel. So he does the next best thing: He remains quiet. If he were to talk, he's afraid he might blow up or say something vicious or hurtful.

Jim also has something else eating at him. Three weeks ago he was made a partner of his law firm. This has meant a bigger salary, a bigger office, and a bigger aura with which to walk the halls. Suddenly, secretaries and office managers and female associates are starting to look at him as they never had before. Cynthia, a striking young graduate of Fordham Law School, poked her head into Jim's office the other day to see if he might like to stroll through the park with her at lunchtime. And this very evening she came by to see if he was in the mood for a drink after work. He was.

Cynthia and Jim sat in a corner booth of a dark bar, downing several drinks and getting mellow. Cynthia leaned her head onto Jim's shoulder. They kissed. Cynthia invited Jim back to her place to cook dinner for him. He refused. Ellen was expecting him. Still, he was mightily tempted.

When Ellen opens the door for him and holds up her pale lips to be kissed, Jim's feelings of dissatisfaction nearly overwhelm him. Who *is* this depressing little woman? Certainly not the creature with whom he is going to have to spend the rest of his life. Not when there are Cynthias out there, younger women, prettier women, bouncier women, thinner women, women who aren't drab and played out and desperate for one's company. Why, it is all Jim can do to be civil to Ellen as they plod through their dinner. Secretly he vows that next time Cynthia proffers herself he will snap her up in an instant. Maybe even move in with her. His life with Ellen has become much too dreary and suffocating. He is a partner in an important law firm now. He doesn't want this dumpy woman at the table with him to drag him down, make his life colorless and sexless and void of romantic promise.

Don't think, of course, that Ellen isn't picking up Jim's feelings. Oh, maybe not consciously. It would be far too painful for her to bear to admit them to herself. But, obviously, something is wrong. The man is just sitting there staring glumly at his plate. And in the pit of her stomach, Ellen is sure that his misery has something to do with her.

"How was your day?" she asks in a meek little voice.

"Okay," Jim answers without further elaboration. Aside from a few additional exchanges of mundane chitchat, the meal ends in silence. The couple repairs to their bedroom.

As Ellen undresses for bed, she feels embarrassed. Her belly, which used to be flat and trim, is now plump, a little mound. Not even a trace of her once shapely waist has yet reappeared. She has promised herself to start doing exercises soon, to cut back on her intake of food. But nursing keeps her too hungry. Oh, well, in six or nine months she will have gotten somewhat used to the routine of having a baby and will begin to work on her figure and her wardrobe again. Meanwhile, she will try to manufacture a little lust, hoping that intercourse will somehow draw her morose husband out of his funk.

Still remaining silent, Jim turns off the light. Ellen lies in bed on her back, staring at the ceiling, thinking that Jim will perhaps take her in his arms. He doesn't.

Reaching out, she takes his hand, holding it tightly. His fingers lie limp in her grasp. Although she doesn't feel even the slightest bit lustful, she snuggles up against him, draping her leg over his. Still he remains unresponsive. To Ellen, the thought of intercourse now is not repugnant, just totally, utterly joyless. Her id is tied up in her nursing. And because she views herself as unattractive, she does not feel sexy, erotic. But she cannot think of any other way to reach Jim, to make him respond to her. And she can't endure going to sleep without first extracting from him some sign that he is still in love with her.

Nevertheless, there is an instinct that what she is about to undertake is self-destructive, means that literally work *against* an end. But, still, she cannot help herself. She feels too alone and unloved in the presence of such icy aloofness. So she climbs atop her husband and begins kissing his neck. After a minute or two he can't help but become stimulated. Soon husband and wife are making love, Jim imagining himself in bed with Cynthia, Ellen wondering why the experience is so much more hollow, so much less cozy than she'd hoped.

When they are finished, Ellen cuddles against Jim's chest. He pats her lightly on the shoulder for a few seconds, then stops, his body as still and quiet as before they'd made love. Ellen gazes into the darkness, a sensation of panic beginning to mount in her chest. Jim also gazes into the night, barely able to keep his arm around his wife, to allow her head to lie on his chest. How pathetic it was of her to have made love with him. Obviously, she hadn't been in the mood. She'd just done it to please him. How desperate! He must make sure to arrange a lunch date with Cynthia immediately upon getting into the office tomorrow. If he doesn't get away from this woeful wife of his soon, he will drown. How did he ever get drawn into this stultifying relationship in the first place?

Now perhaps you're thinking, *How silly of Jim! Doesn't he know that he's feeling this way only because he and his wife have just had a baby? Doesn't he realize that just about every couple that parents a child goes through similar postpartum blues? In another six or nine months Ellen will be as good as new again, sexy and vibrant and alluring.*

And, of course, if that's what you're thinking, you'd be right. It *is* silly, immature, and callow of Jim to feel this way. Yet you'd be stunned at how many millions of people have come to believe that their very first negative response to a relationship must be *trusted*—even worse, acted upon. Marriages tumble down like card houses today because a husband puts on five pounds and no longer looks good in a pair of jeans, because a wife says something dull or trite at a business dinner, embarrassing her husband to the point of no return.

Thus, in the case of Jim and Ellen, there may very well be cause for alarm. Perhaps fifty years ago the concept of divorce or infidelity would never have occurred to a young man in a similar frame of mind. But today these two choices are very real to him. And what's more, to many people they would not even be considered odd or radical. One is tired of one's wife? One splits. Or fools around on the side.

Well, what could or should a woman in Ellen's circumstances do rather than have intercourse with her silent, morose husband? The answer is simple. She must get him to *talk* about what is on his mind, to express his feelings as completely and cathartically as he is able. Only if she succeeds at this is it safe or constructive for her to sleep with him. Otherwise, intercourse is more destructive than healing to the relationship. She is far better off to forego sex with him. He will respect and admire her more for having had the strength to resist reassuring herself of his love through meaningless lovemaking.

Of course, he will respect and admire and become *dependent* on her if she insists that he talk to her. Although he does not realize it, talk—not sex—is what he wants with her now. He wants to express his feelings of discontent and depression, of things being out of kilter between them, not like old times. His feelings of disloyalty are making him miserable. He must let them out in some way, either by expressing them literally—by having an affair, breaking up—or by verbalizing them to the person to whom he is closest. Nothing less than the process of articulating them will help dissipate them, make him feel closer to his mate at this time.

The problem is that in a situation such as this, the woman may be as loath to begin the necessary discussion as the man. He is reluctant to begin talking because to say what is on his mind will be to relive it, to feel it even more intensely for the moment. Also, how can he say such hateful, mean things to his wife? And she is reluctant because she senses that her husband is about to say some hurtful and loveless things to her, things that are going to make her feel bad. *You don't look good anymore. You're too fat. I'm not attracted to you.* And yet she must figure out a way to make him talk. The dialogue must begin. True, it may be acrid-tasting medicine. Yet the disease, and its possible ravages, are far worse.

So we say to you, if you find yourself in a similar situation—getting into bed with a grim, quiet partner— do not use sex to assuage your feelings of being unloved. Make your mate talk to you instead. We know it may not be easy, but nevertheless, you must start a conversation, however wooden, however constipated. And you must forge ahead. Because as difficult and as irrelevant as the situation may seem, you should understand that at any moment you can have a mammoth and heart-warming breakthrough. Know that positive results can come with astonishing ease and quickness.

It is often far simpler to repair a broken marriage than either participant would ever imagine. Let that buoy you when you quake at the prospect of making conversation instead of love. Think: *I am about to make my marriage and myself better, vastly better.* And then do it. Instead of snuggling up next to your mate, say, "What's bugging you?" Often that's all you have to do.

And if he or she doesn't answer, repeat your question. If your mate still won't talk, declare, "Well, then I'm going to sleep. I'm not going to make love with you until we get whatever's troubling you out in the open."

Our experience has been that asking for openness and honesty is frequently enough to get one's mate to begin to open up. The only danger now is that what comes out may be terribly hurtful to you. The following pages show you how you can handle that barrage of words and how even verbal abuse can be a positive sign.

3   Don't Walk on Eggshells

One of the most common reasons people resist attempting to get their mate to talk is that they are afraid of an explosion, an ugly confrontation, loud yelling. We have heard many people characterize the last years of their marriage as "walking on eggshells."

On one level, this sort of pseudo-diplomacy seems to make good sense. Who wants to be hollered at? Who doesn't get intimidated or scared by someone else blowing his stack? And then there are the nameless fears. If I get her really mad, she will tell me what I know she's secretly been thinking all along, that she doesn't love me anymore. He will inform me that he no longer finds me pretty. My mate will storm out the door, never to return. And so rather than risk the discomfort and the turbulent feelings that might accompany a frank and free-flowing verbal exchange, many people tiptoe around a silent, brooding mate and reinforce his or her propensity *not* to open up.

We think this is a mistake. Certainly it is true that raised voices can be frightening, but we can reassure you that in almost all cases your mate's bark will be considerably scarier than his or her bite. Your husband may bellow as loud as a bull; your wife may shriek so loudly the neighbors can hear. But it is unlikely that your mate will resort to physical violence (in a later section we show you how to avoid this possibility) or announce that he or she is leaving on the spot. What will probably happen if you manage to press the right button is that you will unleash an initial onrush of hostility and/or rage that before very long will ease to the point where a more reasoned exchange of feelings and ideas can begin.

The problem, of course, is getting to this point, and to help you accomplish that, we advise you to brace yourself ahead of time not to flee a loud argument. Strengthen your resolve by reminding yourself that this is the only way, that to go around walking on eggshells the rest of your marriage will not make for much of a marriage. Life is short. Relationships do not magically improve with time unless you do something to improve them. Also be aware that your mate's initial explosion will probably last no more than a minute or two. It is simply too physically demanding to go on yelling much longer than that.

And don't argue back angrily yourself. This will only further inflame your spouse. His or her denunciation of you may hurt and enrage you, but console yourself with the knowledge that it is probably far better than a stony silence. Maybe all your spouse needs is to let off a little bile and ire. After you've endured a few minutes of strident verbal attack, you'll be amazed at how harmless it suddenly seems. You'll also be surprised at how rapidly this kind of an explosion can drain your mate's anger and hatred. To express it aloud is often to see it disappear.

Now, we realize that to be the brunt of a thunderous verbal attack may be easier for us to recommend than for you to endure, yet this may be necessary if husband and wife are to keep their relationship intact. One middle-aged man, Carl, reports that it took him years of psychoanalysis to get over his fear of strident screaming. Not surprisingly, his mother was an explosive, fuming woman who would erupt in a torrent of vitriol at the slightest provocation. The sight of her angry, red face (which he can recall at will to this day) appeared loveless, almost murderous, to Carl, and it wounded him terribly to think that his own mother at times seemed to hate him so.

When he was in his early twenties, Carl sought out and married a woman of similar temperament to his mother's. It is well documented that people often seek qualities in their mates that remind them of their parents. It simply didn't seem natural to him not to have the same sense of imminent danger in his home as an adult that had been there as a child. In a certain way, he got more than he'd bargained for. As angry as his mother got, he knew deep down that she would never leave. He wasn't so certain about his wife. This terrified Carl because he doubted that he could ever attract another woman.

As a result, he tiptoed around the house like a wraith, in constant fear that he might inadvertently trigger one of his wife's irrational rages. So painful did this mode of existence become for him that he finally entered psychotherapy. One of the problems he worked on most assiduously was his fear of making his wife angry. It took several years of probing and examining and talking through with his doctor, but eventually he was able to stand his ground and endure his wife's angry screams, no matter how loud they were. When she was through, he would answer calmly and rationally, in a voice calculated to soothe rather than pique her ire. And he came to realize that although he experienced an initial sense of terror at the onslaught of her rage, the tidal wave of screaming was really rather harmless. More importantly, he discovered that the whole process of triggering his wife's anger somehow managed to lay to rest his anxiety that at any moment she might leave him.

It seems that by *refusing* to argue with her, by doing everything in his power to *keep* her from blowing up, he had in effect been damming up her desire to express herself. This woman occasionally needed to scream her lungs out. By frustrating her, Carl had been forcing her anger back on itself. This, in turn, is what made her almost panicky in her desire to get out of the marriage.

What about you? Are you tiptoeing around your home, afraid of rousing a brooding mate into an explosive rage followed by desertion? If so, you have been doing yourself, your mate, and your marriage a disservice. We don't recommend you rush into the den, grab the newspaper out of his or her hands, and hurl epithets at the astonished person sitting there. Out-of-control arguing is to be discouraged at all costs. On the other hand, skulking from one room to another in an attempt to placate a churlish spouse may be worse.

We recommend going about business as usual, saying what you feel like saying (within reason), acting the way you want to act. If you precipitate an angry outburst in your mate, so what? He or she may yell, fume, perhaps even stomp up and down. But so long as he or she does not get physically violent, what is the harm? And at least you've got the makings of a dialogue, which, we will stress over and over again, is the soundest bond we know for holding on to a love.

4   Starting a Dialogue

Time and time again on the preceding pages we have mentioned the importance of getting your mate to talk, to open up, even if it means your having to endure a verbal attack or to engage in an argument.

Many of us have difficulty handling anger of any sort—our spouse's or our own. Even when we do get angry, we often do so ineffectively. We attempt to argue our cause, but we often do little more than yell and scream, or cry in utter frustration. Our anger, in a word, generates more heat than light. In this section we will help you learn to argue more skillfully and effectively.

We will also equip you with several proven techniques for starting a conversation with someone who seems particularly resistant to talking. These are techniques that therapists use in the process of getting a new or especially silent patient to say more, and they have been designed to trigger as much conversation and genuine feeling as possible.

So let's look at a few basic principles of human psychology, and see how they can translate into methods that will work for you. There's nothing tricky or underhanded about any of this, just a more satisfying and effective way to begin to talk.

Avoiding Distance

Stay as close to your spouse as you possibly can. We're talking here about physical proximity. Avoid anything that will keep you apart. You may be the greatest debater in the world, but there's no contest if you can't find your adversary.

If he or she will permit it, touch your spouse. Not sexually. Not erotically. Just gently and caringly to show that you're making contact. If you can't touch, then sit close when you talk. Maintain eye contact. Arguments from one room to the next are a waste of time.

There's no need to be a pest about this. If your spouse is feeling trapped, it will do no good to sit on him when he tries to leave the room. The point is, when you do talk, engage him in a way that commands his full attention. That requires direct contact between the two of you. It does not mean you should spend all day together, sulking in opposite ends of the house.

Framing and Reframing

Criminal lawyers know that cases are won or lost by how they are presented to the jury.

A man is caught breaking into a drugstore. He has one prior conviction for burglary. At the trial, the prosecutor demands a conviction. He talks about the seriousness of the crime. He emphasizes the man's greed and his prior record. He decries the wave of burglaries in town.

The defense attorney takes his turn. He downplays the deed: There was no weapon, and no one was hurt. In a neighborhood known for crime, his client has only one prior conviction. He is active in school athletics. He has a sick wife.

Both lawyers are telling the truth. They are simply focusing on different aspects of reality. They are framing that part of the picture they wish to present. The prosecutor's frame contains the man's ugly side. One sees only his greed and his meanness. The defender's frame includes a scene of family, of community, and of human frailty.

Every point of dispute between you and your spouse is a lot more complicated than you think. There's always some truth to both sides. You cannot hope to sell your view of reality unless you are willing to buy your mate's.

You complain that your husband is boisterous. You've been arguing about his behavior in company. You've framed the problem as his being "uncouth." Now reframe it: "You know, Les, I love the way you're always the life of the party. But sometimes you're too much for my stuffy friends at church. Can you humor them, for me? Then we can both yack it up at the lodge."

You and your wife have been arguing about sex. You think that she's lost interest, so you've framed the scene by calling her frigid. Try reframing it: "We've always had a fantastic love life. For some reason, we've both cooled down. How can we build the fire again?"

Dwell on the best parts of your marriage, even if the best parts have been in the past. Often, simply remembering the good times will tide a couple over its current crisis and offer a vision of how it can be once again. Reminiscing about your shared history helps put events into perspective. A simple statement beginning with "Remember when we bought that Chevrolet," or "when Jeffrey was born," or "when we found our first apartment" will elicit thoughts of happy remembrance and direct the conversation toward a new course.

Everyone who contemplates leaving a marriage has a need to see only the negatives. He or she must do this in order to be able to break away. If the leaver sees the whole picture, both positives and negatives, he or she would find it too painful to go. He would have to admit to his mixed feelings about the marriage, to his wavering and to his indecision. So he denigrates his wife, then he can leave with peace of mind. Tearing her down may seem cruel and unfair, but for him it is actually a form of self-protection.

The truth is, of course, that every intimate relationship has both positives and negatives. Concentrating on the negatives is not dishonest. It is merely one construction of reality. It is one frame. There are many others.

He remembers how much money you blew on your last vacation. You remind him of the fantastic time you both had. She remembers that you yelled at her father before he died. You remind her of your countless trips to the hospital and of how much her father loved you.

Your task, in a word, is to match every negative view with a positive one. And here's the amazing thing: The two views are of the very same event.

Finally, as obvious as it may seem, give credit where credit is due. You'll be astonished at how easily he'll swallow your criticism if you sugar-coat it with your praise. Family therapists call this the kick-and-stroke technique. They use it to kick families who are stuck in a rut. But they praise them at the same time, and the families keep coming back for more.

Joining

Another technique that helps keep a conversation going is to join, or agree with, the other party. You can even go so far as to join in his or her criticism of you. Your husband accuses you of talking about only silly things at the dinner table. Agree with him: "You're right. I do prattle on, don't I?" Your wife complains that you're not bringing home enough money. Concur: "You're right. I'm not earning enough. I feel terrible about that."

A recent *New Yorker* cartoon clearly demonstrates the concept of joining. A thoroughly stern and grouchy-looking man responds to his wife, "I most heartily agree with you, Matilda. If everybody in the world were like me, it would be a dreadful world." It's not pleasant, of course, to put yourself down, but there may be some truth in your mate's criticism of you. And he or she will admire your sagacity in recognizing your fault.

He or she will also be surprised by the self-control you've demonstrated by refusing to be drawn into a silly argument, and will wonder if you're not all of a sudden changing for the better (change is something we discuss at length a little later on).

No matter how much conflict exists in your marriage, there are more areas of agreement than you might imagine. Commonly held views are often buried in the rubble of your battles, and you sometimes have to search and dig them out.

After you define an area of agreement, exploit it. For any given issue, highlight those aspects of the matter where you and your mate see eye to eye. Professional negotiators do this when they resolve an argument. If they can define the territory of common agreement, the disputed area is cut down to size and the fight suddenly looms not quite so large.

If you can agree on nothing else, you and your spouse should at least be able to find someone you both hate. Hostile nations fall into each other's arms if they have a common enemy. (Witness the U.S. and China making up, united in their antipathy toward the Soviet Union.) Hostile spouses also support each other in the face of a common attack. Uniting against a common enemy is an almost foolproof way to bring both nations and people together.

You and your mate can join forces in a noble cause, as when you both used to march to fight segregation or poverty. Or you can forge a common pact against your parents or in-laws. He tells you how miserable your mother made him feel when she visited. You can't agree more. She's an impossible woman. You ought to know! You and he have got to work together to make sure she doesn't come within fifty miles of your door.

Here's another way to keep a conversation going. It's often called echoing. Let us say that in response to your attempt to start a dialogue with her, your wife has

responded, "Leave me alone. You're bothering me."
Must the conversation end right there? Not necessarily. Try repeating her last few words by turning them
into a question. For example, you would say, "I'm
bothering you?"

Your wife may very likely feel compelled to elaborate. "Yeah, I can never sit here in peace and be by
myself and think."

Your response would be, "You just want to sit and
think?" And so on and so on. The process may feel
artificial at first, but don't be surprised if two or three
echoes down the line the conversation has picked up
enough momentum to keep going on its own.

Using Verbal Judo

If you were being attacked by a six-and-a-half-foot
muscleman, you would most likely have the good sense
not to oppose his force with your own counterforce—
unless, of course, you were seven feet tall and even
stronger. You would most likely try to escape or to talk
him out of hitting you.

If you knew judo, though, it would be a very different
story. You might be a lot smaller, but you'd have no
trouble swinging that bully over your head and onto his
rear end.

Some of you, of course, do know judo—or karate or
aikido—and you understand the principles of these
martial arts. At risk of oversimplification, let us state
one basic principle as follows: Never try to block your
opponent's thrust. Simply *redirect* his momentum, and
you'll turn it to your own advantage.

A man comes rushing at you with a knife. You know
judo. You don't try to stop the knife. You know that
you cannot. What you do is catch your attacker at a
fulcrum point and change the direction of the onslaught, and the big lug crashes to the floor like a sack
of bricks. The brute's own might has been used to do
him in.

The very same principle applies in verbal arguments.

Verbal judo is especially useful if you are the underdog. Let's say your husband is sales manager at an automobile dealership. You'll never talk him down. You're the underdog. Or your wife is chief litigation attorney at a criminal law firm. Forget it. You're the underdog. So act accordingly.

How then do you use verbal judo? Just like you use physical judo. Don't oppose your spouse's attack. Redirect it. Use its momentum for your own goals.

The three kids are driving you crazy. He thinks you overprotect them. One day he assaults you with a particularly vicious attack: "I'm sick and tired of the whole lot of you. You can take *your* kids and go to hell."

Your first impulse is to oppose this lout with the old, familiar arguments. They seem to make sense. Except they have never worked before, and they won't work now. "What do you mean, 'your kids'? They're yours, too." Or: "What about your responsibilities as a father and a husband?" Or simply: "You can go to hell, too." Force provokes counterforce.

Try instead some verbal judo. "You're absolutely right, Ted. The little bastards are wrecking our marriage. Let's give them away."

He looks at you stunned, but he can't help smiling. The big lug is in a heap on the floor. He doesn't know what hit him.

Using Flattery

If we can turn the old saying around a bit, don't try to catch your honey with vinegar. Try being sweet instead.

A little flattery never hurts. And the bigger they come, the easier they are to flatter. Perhaps it's a universal human need. People just want to be told how great they are.

Let us say that your husband has on a particularly nice outfit or your neighbor mentions over coffee what a fine sense of humor your wife has. Pass the comment along. To hear a complimentary remark about oneself often eases a person's tension, makes him or her want to hear more. You may find your mate beginning to question you about what else your nice neighbor had to say. From there, it may be relatively easy to slide into conversation about other things.

Let us relate a rather dramatic case history to demonstrate the power of flattery. Simon was a mover. A fast-talking sales manager with lots of cash in his pocket and fancy clothes on his frame, he was used to having his pick of women. And he usually picked the best: willowy, high-fashion ladies with charm and poise.

Then he met Rose. Plain Rose, a clerk in a grocery store. Surely it wasn't her personality or her looks, but there was an inner soul, a warmth, that told Simon that this was *the* woman.

Rose was willing to accept his dates, but she wasn't a bit interested in becoming serious. Sure, he was fun, but she wanted someone more solid. Simon was a dreamer, a *luftmensch,* a builder of castles in the air. Rose was sober and practical. Simon was great for laughs, but as a husband—forget it.

One day, Simon invited Rose to go canoeing with him in the country. She had already decided to end the relationship, but she had never canoed before and could not resist the chance. So she accepted this last date.

It was a beautiful fall day. Simon brought his banjo and his straw hat. Romance was in the air, but not for Rose. When Simon asked her to marry him, for the hundredth time, she knew she had had enough. She decided to let him have it.

"You want to know what I think of you? You are the vainest man I have ever met. You're egotistical and self-centered. You don't have a serious bone in your body. You're uneducated and crude. You're just a bag of hot air. I wouldn't marry you if you were the last man on earth."

Simon did not blink.

"Then let me tell you what I think of you. You are

the finest woman on the face of the earth. You are unspeakably beautiful. You're sensitive and intelligent. I am in awe of your charm. Your glow nourishes my soul."

Rose wept and embraced Simon.

They were married at City Hall the next week.

Fighting Fairly

Don't use dirty tricks. Whatever their short-term advantages, they're bound to backfire and reduce you in your spouse's esteem.

Try to win the argument, not to trounce your opponent. Or else you might win the battle and lose the war. Scoring points is not important, because no one is keeping count. When you feel that you've made your point, be gracious. Don't humiliate him. Leave her a face-saving out.

Similarly, don't try to corner your spouse. No one likes to be trapped. He or she may have to concede the point but will end up being bitter and resentful. Even if you think you are holding a trump card, play it cautiously.

You suspect that your wife has been cheating on you. One evening you chance to see her drive by with a strange man. You think you've got the goods on her. Be careful. Don't confront her with photographs, old telephone bills, or sworn affidavits. You're not in a courtroom. Better to tell her gently that she seems to have shifted her affection elsewhere and that you don't approve. You wish she would come back to you so the two of you can begin to work things out.

Never, never, never use the kids as pawns. It's not fair to the kids, and it doesn't work. Burdening the children with your problems might provide some temporary comfort, but nothing is more certain to disgrace you in your spouse's eyes.

Be careful with friends, parents, and in-laws. You can seek them out for help and advice, but be certain not to embarrass your spouse or to violate his or her confidence. Secrets between you and your spouse are sacred and should not be divulged for some short-term gain. You may, for example, tell your best friend or your mother-in-law that your husband does not appreciate your cooking. You may not tell them that he is having trouble performing in bed.

Don't sulk. Pouting children are not popular, and pouting adults, even less so. Communicate your problems with words. Don't attempt to make him feel guilty by demonstrating with your expressions how miserable you are. A sourpuss will drive him or her out, if nothing else will.

Being Specific and Positive

While arguments can serve to get a lot of feeling off your chest, screaming and shouting generally accomplish little. On the other hand, arguments actually can be quite constructive if they succeed in enhancing communication or in reducing conflict between two people.

The trick to arguing constructively is to be specific and positive. You need to focus on what the conflict is really about. Identify the problems as you see them as clearly as possible, and try to maintain an optimistic approach. You are interested in solving disputes and developing a plan of action, not in hitting your spouse over the head with a bag of gripes.

Tell your mate what you want. Simply declare: "I would like you to talk to me more." There is little here that your spouse can fly off the handle about, for it is nothing more than a statement of your desire for more communication. Don't blame. Do *not* say: "You never talk to me anymore." That is an attack.

Avoid imputing motivation to your spouse's actions. In other words, while you may criticize his behavior, don't attempt to psychoanalyze it. You can tell your wife that she spoils the children. Don't tell her that she does so because she's a spoiled child herself.

If you think your marriage is in trouble, try to

approach your spouse openly and without defensiveness. You might ask something like: "What is it that you need that you're not getting in this marriage?" Such a question calls for specific and positive suggestions. It does not encourage your spouse to dwell on the negatives.

If things have reached the point that she's threatened to leave, you might ask: "What do I have to do to keep you from leaving?" Or: "I love you. Give me a list of the things I must change." Statements like these may actually make your mate uncomfortable, because they toss the ball squarely into his court. On the other hand, they convey to him that you are deadly serious about doing what has to be done, and you need to know how to go about doing it.

Don't be afraid to ask for help, even if you believe your spouse is no longer inclined to help you. You might say: "I need your help to be able to change. Help me learn what I must do."

Just as you have been specific, you have a right to expect specific answers from your spouse. Responses like "You've got to clean up your act if you want me to stay," or "You've got to stop acting like a ninny" are of no value. Politely but firmly continue to demand specifics. "What must I do to clean up my act?" "Exactly how do you expect me to behave?" "What specifically do you want me to do?"

Eventually, you will get the information you need. Even more important, perhaps, your mate will get the message that you're developing a plan and you expect it to work. He will get the idea that there may be some real hope, for the first time.

Being Flexible

We all know that there are many ways to go about solving a problem. If we get stuck, we try to be flexible and inventive. Yet, with marital difficulties, most of us do just the opposite. The tougher the problem, the narrower and more rigid we become.

We behave this way, of course, to protect ourselves from getting hurt. But while withdrawing into one's shell may offer some degree of emotional protection, it does little for communication or for problem solving. When you and your spouse have come to an impasse, this is precisely the time to be open-minded and creative.

As with any other puzzle, marital problems must be considered from all angles. Old, unworkable solutions must be discarded and more novel approaches tried. Blame should be avoided. We realize it is well nigh impossible to be completely open and undefensive in the midst of marital turmoil. But you often need to be just a little less stubborn to break through to your mate, just a bit more creative to spark his or her natural warmth. Rest assured, the warmth is there, probably in much greater abundance than you've come to believe. Perhaps all it takes to unlock it is a slightly *different* key.

While we're on the subject of blame, let us caution you against too much self-righteousness. You may be missing something important but not realize it. Before you know it, you're locked into a position that you don't want. There is probably nothing more frustrating than knowing you no longer believe your own arguments but being in too deep to turn back.

Remember that you can always cut your losses. There is no law requiring you to defend a point of view you would really like to abandon. "You know, Liz, I think I've been a real horse's ass about this. You're completely right. Forget I ever brought it up."

Try to avoid so-called symmetrical power struggles. That's a fancy term for arguments that sound like: "Yes, I do." "No, you don't." At every step, each side ups the ante and screams louder. Obviously, nothing is accomplished. If you find yourself in a symmetrical power struggle, get out of it. Declare a recess. Say something weird. Stand on your head.

If you're really flexible, you might occasionally dabble with a bit of reverse psychology, although we advise you to use it with caution. Family therapists speak of using "paradoxical" techniques.

Your husband spends each Friday night at the bar and you resent it mightily. Since nothing else has worked, try suggesting that he spend both Friday *and* Saturday nights swilling it down. Your wife visits her mother twice a week. Suggest that her mother move in.

The idea behind the paradox is that the individual will recoil from the logical consequences of his behavior and end up doing just the opposite of what you suggest. Reverse psychology is not for the lily-livered. It can backfire. But if you really have a feel for what you're doing, you may be remarkably successful. Otherwise, we suggest that you be creative but that you stick with more straightforward techniques.

Avoiding Physical Violence

Physical violence, unfortunately, is a real fact in no small number of marriages. We have tried to consider every other issue from a nonsexist perspective, but no one can deny that physical violence is almost exclusively a male-against-female phenomenon.

A single blow lashed out in anger is not wife abuse. But we want to prevent even this, and, in a moment, we will consider how. At the outset, though, let us be quite categorical. *Physical violence is completely unacceptable*. If you are a battered wife, you do not need this book. You need a lawyer, a cop, and a district attorney.

We have explored many techniques for starting a dialogue, some of which involve bluntness and even provocation. How do you keep from pushing him too far? Mainly, you use common sense.

Has your husband ever been violent before? We are quite aware of the statistics on battered women, but the fact is that the large majority of men are not wife abusers. If your husband has never hit you or anybody else, it is unlikely that he is going to start now.

Between the extremes of violent and nonviolent men, however, is a sizable group in the middle. These men do not hit, as a rule, but can be pushed over the brink. He may not have struck out at you before, but you have sensed in the past that he has come awfully close. Here is what to do.

First, you and he must agree at the outset that there will be no physical violence. Ask him to tell you when to back off. "Frank, I love you very much, and I'm not going to sit by while our marriage falls apart. I insist on talking to you and discussing the issues between us. Tell me if I push you too hard, and I'll stop. But we've got to agree that there will be no violence."

Be aware of what is going on in his life, and don't press him when he is under stress. If he has just had a run-in with his boss, don't insist on discussing your sexual difficulties. Don't attempt to dialogue if he is unduly anxious or tired or sick. To turn the tables a minute, don't attempt to argue with your wife if she's got bad premenstrual pain and is climbing the walls.

Don't argue with your mate if he or she is drunk. Or if *you* are drunk. We see no point in holding a conversation under any circumstances with someone who is intoxicated. The large majority of violent crimes occur among people who are drinking. If he is drunk, he might become nasty, and chances are that he won't remember what you fought about anyway after he sobers up. If he slugs you, he is sure to regret it the next day. But such an occurrence, in addition to being dangerous, will surely embitter both of you and drive you further apart.

Avoid personal attacks. Keep the argument as issue-oriented and as free of personalities as possible. Agree in advance that, if the argument becomes too heated, either of you can ask for "time out," and the other will respect it. Don't try to get everything resolved in one session. Marathon arguments are rarely useful.

Don't corner him or push him to the wall. Never insult his manhood, particularly if he is sensitive on that point. Avoid feminist rhetoric. Nothing seems to inflame men these days as much as being the brunt of a feminist assault.

Be aware of what has triggered him to overreact before, and avoid it. Watch for obvious signs of anger and impending loss of control. These signs differ for each individual. You may have learned from long experience that the tic in his right eye means he is highly anxious. Shouting, sweating, pacing the floor, gooseflesh, and dilated pupils—the so-called fight-or-flight reaction—are all signs of high degrees of arousal and anxiety.

Finally, consider having another person accessible if either of you feels out of control. Agree on it in advance. "You trust your brother Tom. Can we call him down to referee, or at least to make sure that we don't clobber one another?"

Needless to say, none of these techniques can work magic. For them to be truly effective, you've got to be infinitely gentle, patient, persevering, and resolute in their application. And as you've probably already surmised, more than a few of them can be used in combination. When executed wisely, they can have an enormous influence in getting a good dialogue started.

5   Listening

There's an old joke that psychiatrists tell among themselves.

A young man runs into his former therapist in an elevator. "Tell me, Doc," he asks. "How in the world do you put up with your work? All day long you listen to people's troubles. You listen to their troubles with work and their problems at home. You sit there all day and listen to all those struggles and worries. How do you do it?"

As the elevator doors begin to open, a small smile creases the old professional's beard, and he looks the young man squarely in the eye.

"Who listens?"

Any good therapist, of course, does listen. But what about you? Listening is hard work. An awful lot harder than talking. We human beings would rather talk than listen. It's human nature.

Just watch children in a classroom. The smaller ones go on and on, fairly oblivious to what the other kids are saying. As they get older, kids learn from teachers and then from their peers that talking all the time doesn't make you very popular, because everyone else wants to talk. So kids learn gradually to stop talking and to let the others have a chance. But to stop talking is only the first step and the easiest one. Listening—*really* listening —is a much tougher skill to develop.

A few pages back we spoke about the need to get your mate to talk, and we gave you a number of suggestions on how to get started. But what if your mate remains resolute in not opening up to you, in refusing to begin dialogue? Our question, then, is: Are you really listening?

Listening, you must understand, is a lot more than simply sitting there in silence, just as thinking is more than staring into space. Both listening and thinking are intense, active processes. Both take a little self-discipline, and both pay handsome rewards. In fact, once you become a really skilled listener, you will have the tools to get even the most determinedly silent mate to talk.

But before we discuss how to listen, let us first paint a picture of what can happen when you *don't* listen.

Pat and Harry have been married for twelve years. They have three children. Harry is a witty, athletic, clever, and enormously talented executive who makes well over $50,000 a year. Over the past decade, Pat has done some volunteer work with the PTA in town, but most of her time has been devoted to her children. Both husband and wife are trim and tall and extremely attractive. They keep in shape by jogging and playing racket sports.

At parties, Harry is known for his ability to keep an entire assemblage laughing and drinking and dancing until the wee hours of the morning. Pat is known for her smashing, revealing outfits, which never fail to show off her willowy figure to its best advantage. Few men in their crowd, however, ever actively flirt with Pat because she has always seemed almost slavishly devoted to her husband, and most of the men feel inadequate next to Harry, such is the power and charm of his personality. And yet, just several months before their twelfth anniversary, Pat informed Harry that she was leaving him for another man.

Everyone in their neighborhood was stunned and could hardly wait to see who had lured this extraordinarily pretty woman away from her dynamo of a husband. An actor? A senator? A foreign diplomat? All were agreed that whoever it was must be someone special. They were wrong. It was Mr. L., the owner of a dry-cleaning store in town, a man far less prepossessing in almost every way than Harry: shorter, balder, rounder, poorer, and vastly less entertaining. Yet he had one talent Harry lacked: He listened, *really* listened, and this is what attracted Pat to him.

For the past two or three years, Pat had been going through a mild emotional crisis. Her children were all in school, full-time, leaving more and more of her daytime hours free and unoccupied. It was unnerving. There was only so much jogging and tennis playing a woman could do. Each day there were long stretches of time when she had literally to look for something to do around the house. It made her feel inadequate. She tried to tell Harry, but he didn't really seem to be listening. Oh, he cocked his head, and looked at her, and nodded sympathetically, and said he'd give her problem some thought. But the vibrations he sent out said, *Oh, come on. Stop making a mountain out of a molehill. You've got a maid, money, clothes, a Mercedes, a pool. What's your problem?* And then Harry was off to a squash game or a round of golf or a board meeting, telling jokes, entertaining, bringing others alive with his energy and his sense of adventure. And Pat found herself increasingly alone with her fear and anxiety and sense of uselessness.

Then she met Mr. L., who had a sad, sympathetic cast to his eyes, as if he were really listening. And the more she revealed, the more he seemed to pay attention, no matter what she told him.

As you might have guessed, much of what she talked about was Harry: how she found it difficult to communicate her feelings to him, how there seemed to be no depth to their relationship, and how she felt ashamed to burden him with her petty troubles since, on the surface anyway, their life together seemed so perfect. Thus, before long, her clandestine meetings with Mr. L. became addictive, nourishing, life-sustaining, for by listening he was validating her sense of self-worth, her very existence.

Naturally, everyone found it mind-boggling to learn that Pat was leaving Harry for the quiet, unassuming Mr. L. Their marriage indeed had seemed so ideal. And unless one, via hindsight only, really thought about it, there was very little reason to believe that Pat and Harry weren't totally happy with one another.

Harry pleaded with Pat to take him back, vowing to change, although still not really sure of what he'd done wrong, what it was that Pat wanted from him. But it was too late. Pat had already switched her emotional allegiance and found her new relationship with her less glamorous lover vastly more satisfying than her marriage.

Now we are aware that some of you might be thinking: *Was Mr. L. really listening? Or was he just pretending to in order to woo Pat away from her husband?* That's an excellent question. Because ultimately, listening is much more than mere public relations.

You have to listen because there are things you have to know. It's amazing how some women will search for long blonde hairs and compromising notes, and how some men will look for hints and scrounge for clues. Yet everything they have to know is right under their very noses. All they have to do is listen. No sneaking. No dishonesty. Your spouse will tell you everything you need to know if you'll only remove your earplugs.

How do you listen without getting a graduate degree in clinical psychology? That's like asking how to exercise when you've never exercised before. There's no question that listening takes some effort and some discipline, but anyone can learn how to do it. And anyone who wants to win back a love *must* do it.

How to Listen

Hearing involves only the use of your ears. To really *listen*, you must also get your brain into gear. Listening, as we have said, is an active process. It involves focusing attention, much like focusing a strong search-light. You can brightly illuminate what you want to highlight and leave everything else in the dark.

Sounds are always competing for your ear. Every individual chooses what he wants to hear and leaves the rest as pure background noise. This is because we human beings, unlike computers, have only a very limited capacity to take in new information at any given time.

"But I want to win back my straying husband or my wandering wife," you say. "Why the spiel on how people hear?" Slow down. If you're impatient after reading a half-page, we would wager that you're even more impatient when your spouse says a half-sentence.

To listen, you must first slow down. In fact, you must stop. Stop talking. Stop fidgeting. Stop letting your mind wander. Focus your attention like a searchlight—no, like a laser beam—on what your husband or wife is saying to you. Block out everything else.

You are an audience of one in a theater. Your spouse is onstage. He or she talks. You listen but in a way you have never listened before. Are your children walking in and out of the room? You wouldn't tolerate that in a theater. Don't accept it at home. "Mary, I want very much to hear what you're about to say. It will help a lot if we ask the children to leave."

Is the TV set on? Does the phone keep ringing? If that happened in the theater, the show would close after opening night. Are the chairs uncomfortable so that, try as you might, you keep thinking of your lower back? Is the newspaper in sight and open to the sports page with the latest results? Bad for theater and the kiss of death for conversation. Your spouse has the stage, and the spotlight is on her. You're the audience, but you're also the stage manager. It's your job to set the stage so that you can sit back and hear.

You'd be surprised how many people say they're prepared to listen and then set up a sideshow to distract everyone's attention. Sort of like throwing a grenade off to the left so the enemy doesn't see you coming. But we're not trying to make war. We're trying to make a lasting peace and finally even love.

"Yes, dear, I'd love to know what you think about my mother, but I hear the kids screaming in the other room." Or: "Yes, go on, but I think my cooking's burning." We know a man who wears a hearing aid that always seems to go on the fritz when his wife is talking. "I can't hear you! Talk louder! That damned hum!" The fellow keeps a secret stock of fresh batteries—pops one in every time his wife is out of town and he's out *on* the town. Some woman propositions him in a singles bar and whispers softly into his bad ear. "You want to meet me at the Holiday Inn on Thirty-sixth Street, room five sixteen, at nine-forty?" Quick as a wink he replies, "You're on!"

A medical miracle? Nonsense. We hear what we want to hear. And we hear what we pay attention to.

And so, a brief review for your post-graduate degree in hearing physiology: (1) Slow down and stop talking; (2) set the stage. Spotlight off you and on your mate; (3) no distractions. Make them go away; and (4) pay attention. You may not like math, but you're not going to graduate unless you hear the teacher and prepare for the exam. Now you've really got to listen as you've never listened before because you're preparing for one of the most important tests of your life.

How to See

All right. You've learned to listen. Now you've got to learn to see. That's not as easy as it sounds. Most freshman law students are exposed to an exercise that goes something like this: A couple of actors are brought into the classroom, and they immediately act out a brief scene—a holdup, for example. The fledgling lawyers are then asked, one by one, to describe what they just saw.

The results are absolutely predictable. Each student reports seeing something quite different. All have reasonably normal eyesight, so these results have nothing to do with vision. The differences are purely the results of the mind-set of the viewer. Student A thinks that the robber had curly black hair. Student B saw his hair as blond and straight. Student C saw a beard, Student D a moustache, and Student E no facial hair at all. Some students saw a gun, some a knife, and some a blackjack.

If there is that much confusion among trained observers looking at objective acts, you can imagine how difficult it is for us to have 20/20 vision in the midst of marital warfare. Under the calmest of conditions we tend to see what we want to see. When emotions run high, we might as well be looking into mirrors in a fun house. Anger or hatred can actually distort faces before your eyes, making them contorted and grotesque. At times of high tension, the most innocent or even conciliatory gesture on the part of your spouse can be seen as an attack.

So, the first thing to recognize about seeing is that your eyes can play tricks. Especially in the heat of passion. Don't believe everything you see or take all that you see at face value. If you've become convinced that your wife is having an affair, every little thing you see will confirm your suspicion. If you are certain that your husband is completely turned off, you will miss his small initiatives. You will see all of his behavior as angry and off-putting. Don't always trust your eyes.

Many therapists use videotape to record themselves and their patients. The patient and even the therapist are often surprised at seeing themselves and seeing what actually took place. It might be nice if we could tape-record our marital disputes and then review the tapes when tempers have cooled. Most of us can't very well do that, but there are a few close substitutes.

Two heads are better than one, and four eyes are better than two. Go right to the enemy's camp. Ask your wife what she saw during your last dispute, and you might be surprised. You looked to her like a raving maniac, and she says she was scared stiff! Impossible. You thought you were as cool as a cucumber. You didn't know you could scare a flea. Ask your husband. He saw you as cold and aloof. Cold? Was he blind to the tears streaming down your cheeks?

Ask other people who know you and who have observed you. But first tell them that you insist that they be objective, not supportive. "Bob, what do you see when you see Alice and me arguing? Please don't give me a pat on the back and tell me what a saint I am. I am blind. I need your eyesight. I must know what you really see."

You don't want to be the emperor or the empress and have all your friends tell you how well you dress. If you are not wearing clothes, you'd better know it and know it fast. Your closest girlfriend tells you that your husband is a male chauvinist pig "just like all the rest of them." So all men are male chauvinist pigs? How does that help you in your struggle to keep your husband? Tell your girlfriend to save the feminist rap for the women's consciousness-raising group. Unless you're prepared to give up completely on the opposite sex, tell her that you need her help in keeping your own male chauvinist from leaving the pigpen. If she can help you see more clearly, maybe you can help him oink a different tune.

As useful as it is to enlist the eyes of others, it is even more important to learn to sharpen your own vision, to learn to see what is really happening and not just what you expect to see.

The quickest road to seeing yourself and your spouse as you really are is to use a little mental sleight-of-hand. Psychiatrists call this technique observing ego, but we'll call it Being Two Places at the Same Time. Imagine that you are a fly on the ceiling looking at two angry people in a heated argument. You recognize both of them—you and your spouse—but you look at them without passion. Your attitude is one of mild curiosity. The last thing in the world you'd want to do is to take sides.

What fools these mortals be! There you are, face red and neck veins bulging. No wonder she thinks you're a potential wife beater and is ready to hightail it out of there for self-preservation. Anyone would be scared. Wait a minute—who's that lady with the granite-stone face? Hold on. That's me. So that's why he calls me sourpuss. Just think. It seems like yesterday I had been voted most popular woman in my college graduating class, and now I look like the Wicked Witch of the West.

To sum up this crash course in learning to see: (1) realize that your vision is often distorted, especially in the cold or the heat of passion; (2) question what you see. Your eyes may be deceiving you; (3) enlist the help of others to tell you what they see, not to tell you what they think you want to hear; and (4) distance yourself from the action. Pretend that you are in the audience, watching yourself and your spouse onstage. At one moment your sympathies are here, at another there. You may still not see everything, but you'll end up with a much better idea of what the show is about.

How to Put It Together

Now that you've learned to listen and to see, you're ready to put it all together. Now that you have the tools for understanding—and these are very powerful tools indeed—you are prepared to act and react to your spouse, and to do it effectively.

Your wife says that she cannot stand your mother. She has said that only ten thousand times before, but you never took her seriously. Everyone has mother-in-law problems. Besides, Mom is seventy-two; how can anyone dislike a harmless old woman? Mom has lived with you for the last five years, since Dad died. You know, of course, how difficult it is for two women to share the same kitchen. But your wife can't be serious that she's about to pack her bags if Mom is not sent to a nursing home.

Okay. Now you're going to try to listen. You set the stage and turn the microphone over to your wife. "What's the use?" she asks. "I've said it ten thousand times before."

"Try it once again," you reply. "The kids are away. The TV's off. Mom is visiting her brother. I'm thinking of nothing but you. I'm going to make an honest effort to hear you."

"All right," she sighs. "I'll try it for the ten thousand and first time. Your mother was always a difficult woman. Your brother and your sister know that. She never liked me, but she is your mother, and so I never complained. Maybe I should have. I tried to make you proud of me and to be a good daughter-in-law. Besides, I respect her for who she is and because she's your mother.

"The situation was certainly tolerable as long as your father was alive. Dad and I knew what a self-centered person Mother is, and we were able to confide in each other and cry on each other's shoulders. Besides, she and your father fought so much that she never had much time to intrude on our life.

"With Dad's death, all that changed. I tried to tell you that I didn't think your mother could live happily with us, but you didn't take me seriously. Maybe I should have been more insistent. Well, you don't know what life around here has been like since Mom moved in. How could you know? You come home after she's locked herself in her room for the night. You're not here during the day, all day, when she carps at me and criticizes you and undercuts our family.

"I've tried to tell you so many times, but you were never willing to listen. I don't want to force you to choose between me and her. I suppose you have your responsibilities. But my sanity is even more important to me than my marriage. And I'm going crazy. So I've had it. It's too late. We're finished."

You sit there stunned. She *has* said it all before, but it

never really registered. Whenever Anne tried to discuss your mother, you'd remember an important business meeting or decide it was time to start disciplining
the children. Or you told her that it couldn't be as bad
as she described. Now, for the first time, you hear what
she's been saying all along.

You also try to see, and you're moved beyond words
at what you see. Your once-young wife has aged fifteen
years in the last five. The luster has gone from her hair,
and the lines are deep in her face. It is crystal clear to
any fool who cares to look that she is not the self-
centered princess you have depicted her to be. She is
talking from her heart. She is mighty angry. But
behind that anger you can see her deep pain and her
guilt.

The tears in your eyes are the first signal to her that
she has made an impact. Maybe she is not totally alone
in the world, slowly going crazy. There is probably
nothing so frustrating as not being heard, as screaming
in the dark. But you've begun to listen, to see, and to
understand. Maybe it's not too late to change.

Any student of human communication knows that
listening can sometimes be tricky business. Take tone
of voice, for example. You ask your employee how he
feels. "Fine," he replies. Said brightly, he means that
he's all right. Said softly and hesitatingly, he probably
means "Fine, I suppose. Are you really interested?"
Said snidely and with sarcasm, your worker is saying,
"Lousy. What do you expect?"

Sometimes you make a sincere attempt to listen, but
you simply do not understand. Your husband seems to
be talking Greek. No one wants to appear stupid, so it's
a normal tendency to pretend to comprehend when you
really do not or when you do a little but not very much.
Confess your ignorance. Tell him that you want to
know what he's saying, but that you're truly confused.
If he believes that you're sincere—that you truly want
to know—he'll translate.

Let's summarize what therapists know about listening. Listening is hard work. It's an active process, involving more than the use of your ears. You must slow down and pay attention. You must stop talking. And you must be observant.

Many people think that they have to give advice or become a problem solver in order to be useful. Experienced therapists know differently. Expert listening is often enough. If the problems are permitted to be expressed, the paths to solutions will often emerge by themselves.

We've spent a good deal of time talking about listening, seeing, and understanding, which are as important to meaningful communication as eggs, flour, and yeast are to making dough. You don't need to become an expert at these skills any more than you need to be a master chef to turn out decent meals at home. If you can improve just 10 percent, you'll get over the hump and be prepared for some of the following specific techniques that can help you win back a love.

How to Probe Gently but Relentlessly

Okay, you've employed some of the preceding techniques to dismantle your mate's silence, and—miracle of miracles—they're working. You and your spouse have begun a dialogue. Your life together is not yet like Romeo and Juliet's, of course, but at least some of the tension, the hostility, the misunderstanding, between you has begun to ebb.

Wonderful. But we must now caution you not to sit back and rest on your laurels because you have got your mate to open up once. Because during a troubled time in a marriage, the abscess keeps reforming, the dialogue must be continuing and ongoing. Encouraging your mate to talk may be a process you have to continue the rest of your life. Your spouse may show annoyance at the onset of yet another "talk session," but he or she will secretly admire your doggedness and commitment to the relationship. More than that, your spouse will welcome the opportunity to open up. The exercise is both depression-lifting and life-giving.

In fact, for many couples we know, talking has become addictive. The reason is simple. They have found the process of lowering their defenses, of expressing their fears and dislikes and doubts, to be so helpful in solving not only marital problems but career and childrearing problems as well, that they find they are living a far smoother, more successful life all around. So, even if your wife flinches at the sight of you walking into the den where she's retreated to be alone with the newspaper, your face creased with that characteristic let's-have-a-talk expression, don't be dissuaded. Say, "Let's talk," anyway. And even if your husband rolls over in bed, flicks out the light, and pulls the blanket over his shoulder, persist. Get the ball rolling, the discussion started. The results will far outweigh any discomfort you may initially feel.

6   The Power of Words

You would be amazed at how many married people seem to expect their partners to read their minds. We're not talking about the wayout fringe that believes in ESP. We're talking about Mr. or Mrs. Rational-in-Everything-Else, who somehow thinks that his or her spouse should have powers of mental telepathy.

Many husbands and wives feel that they don't have to say what is on their minds, since their spouses ought to know what they are thinking. What's more, if they have to say what they want, it no longer counts. "If he doesn't know what I need, then forget it. If I have to tell him, he might as well not do it."

Pat and Tony are a young couple who came for therapy. They agreed to seek help provided they did not have to sit in the room together. They both said they were too embarrassed. Pat's major complaint was that Tony didn't satisfy her in bed. "He only knows one way to do it," she said. "He gets his rocks off and then falls asleep, leaving me unsatisfied and angry. He doesn't seem to care what I want."

Exit Pat and enter Tony. "She comes from a rigid Catholic family. They're all against anything except the missionary position. No oral sex. No touching or anything else. Now, I'm no missionary. I'd had lots of experience before we married, but I don't think Pat wants to hear about it. So I've given up what I enjoy, and it's pretty much cut and dried. But she's still complaining."

Exit Tony and enter Pat. "My family is plenty strict, and that's one reason I married Tony. His family is Catholic, too, but they're much more liberal. I know Tony had a lot of girlfriends in college. He wasn't Most Popular Man on Campus for nothing. I considered myself quite fortunate when he chose me. But now I can't understand why the other women gnashed their teeth with envy. He's a dud in bed. I'm an absolute sexual adventurer compared to him."

The problem here is obvious. He thinks that she's inhibited, and she thinks that he's inhibited. They both have so much respect for the other that they won't chance hurting the other's feelings. Fortunately, they came for help. This sort of problem usually ends up in a series of extramarital affairs, with both partners ultimately feeling unheard and disillusioned.

The longer couples have been married, the more they tend to believe in mind reading. It is true, of course, that by your golden anniversary, you ought to know how he likes his eggs cooked. But people's needs are constantly changing, and no one in a marriage can always read the other's mind. Furthermore, asking for something doesn't make it any less valuable. This business of "If I have to ask, I don't want it" has no place in a mature relationship. You simply must make your needs known and encourage your mate to do the same.

When a marriage is in trouble, of course, partners are less inclined to say what they are thinking. They feel defensive. They are hurt. They have stopped trusting. They tend to keep their own counsel. Strangely enough, though, the belief in mind reading goes on.

"He ought to know how pissed off I am" is a common response. "He knows how he's been behaving. He must know how I feel." It is hard for her to realize that he is just as angry, that he feels just as wronged, and that he believes his emotions are just as obvious.

There may be a great deal of screaming and accusing, but true thoughts—even angry thoughts—are often jealously guarded. Perhaps these true or angry thoughts are suppressed because you don't want to blow your final shots or you want to save them for the divorce court. Or maybe you feel that talking is just a waste of breath.

If angry thoughts are held back, loving ones are kept under absolute lock and key. Your husband is alienated. He is questioning the marriage. He thinks he has no more affection for you and hints that he may leave. Your mind is filled with anger and hurt. But you're also aware of loving thoughts deep down.

Wait for a particularly bitter moment of fighting and recrimination. Then try the following: "You know, David, I really love you." That's all. You may not believe it. It seems absurd. You surely don't believe it before you say it. But the *words themselves* somehow change things. They become more credible to both you and him after they have crossed your lips. (The very same thing happens, in the opposite direction, when you say things that are angry and hateful. Even if you were unsure before, you'll become convinced of your dislike when you speak the wrathful words.)

There are some marital therapists who actually put words into their patients' mouths. They tell them how to act and what to say, no matter what they think or how they feel. The theory behind this therapy is that it makes little difference how people expect to feel about saying something. Most people feel what they say *only after they have said it.*

A couple comes into the session glowering at one another. They sit on opposite ends of the room, separated by three children. They talk to each other through the therapist or through the kids. When they do speak directly, it is in angry monosyllables.

After a few sessions of this, the therapist orders the

partners to sit next to each other. He instructs each partner to smile when he or she talks to the other. He then instructs the husband to take his wife's hand, and then to tell her that he loves her.

The therapist does not ask the man if he feels love for his wife. He never asks a question that might provoke an answer he does not want to hear. What the therapist is doing is pure staging, and he readily admits it. The husband thinks that the words will choke in his throat. Even if he can get them out, he is sure his wife will retch.

The man has no choice. So he takes his wife's hand and he says, "Cindy, I really love you." We know, of course, that he is an actor here, and he is simply reading his lines. But reading lines tends to affect an actor, even a professional one. Just saying "I love you," at home or onstage, loosens something up. You don't believe the words at all before you say them. Once they cross your lips, though, you find that it's no blasphemy. You start to believe them maybe just a little. And so does she. But that's a little more than before.

Let us take this one step further. Believe it or not, the actual words you use make very little difference. Words often are simply the vehicles for ideas, and there are a thousand different ways to phrase the same notion. In psychiatry, these two concepts are called content and process. "Content" denotes the actual words, and "process," the underlying idea. We can infer that the process between A and B is an angry one whether A is calling B a jerk, a nasty fellow, or a no-good-son-of-a-bitch.

You can see that content is less important than process. Therefore, we would advise you not to get too hung up in putting together exactly the right words. Searching for the precise phrasing will inhibit you and might even prevent you from speaking up at all. You'll end up having to say the same thing many different ways in any case, so your choice of words can be rough and approximate the first time around. The clumsiest word has infinitely more power to communicate than the most finely honed thought that never gets expressed.

The important thing is that you translate your feelings and your thoughts into words. In that way, you'll get the process going. Futile attempts at mind reading will stop, and communication will begin. As you use them, your words will become more precise and will better come to represent your thoughts. What is going on between you will then be open and aboveboard. Your words will impact upon your spouse; unexpressed thoughts usually do nothing but create distance.

The Power of the Written Word

Before we leave the issue of effectively expressing your thoughts, let us say a few things about the written word. Obviously, most communication among friends and family members takes place by talking to one another. And most of the advice we have given up until now refers to the use of speech. But there is a place for the written word as well.

Many of you wrote love letters to your mate when you were courting. We are sure you didn't write to save the price of a call. Everyone knows that the written word has a unique power to communicate. While speech floats through the air and then is gone, the impact of a letter is indelible.

The words "I love you," for example, take on a different dimension when committed to paper. If they come from the one you love, you'll read them and reread them and then read them again. People carry love letters with them to the ends of the earth or store them away in their most secret cache. Whether they pull them out every ten minutes or every ten years, the letters continue to produce a lasting magic.

We all know that news conveyed by letter tends to make a greater impact than the spoken word. Good or bad, the facts stand out before your eyes and become imprinted on your brain. A letter cannot easily be ignored.

Letters have other advantages as well. They are written in private and read in private. Therefore, you can think through what you wish to say, relatively unaffected by the heated emotions between you and your spouse. And he or she can read it privately as well, without having to react at that moment. A letter may provoke a strong and even immediate response, but it forces you to reflect a bit before committing yourself to a reply.

Writing is particularly valuable if you do not have the facility for instantly putting your thoughts into cogent words. Even if you pride yourself on your ordinary powers of speech, you may be too angry or too hurt to say exactly what you mean. Responding in a letter, on the other hand, gives you as much time as you need to gather your thoughts.

A letter also allows you the chance to organize your thoughts. Now, we do not believe in the commonly given advice to list the pros and cons, or to tick off the advantages and disadvantages of your marital situation. If you don't know why you want to save your marriage by this time, no amount of list making is likely to help.

On the other hand, putting your best case down in black and white forces you to consider the soundness of your cause. Do your arguments seem as reasonable on paper as they do to your ear? Are you coming across loud and clear? What about the gaps in your own logic? You can examine the weak points in your case, think them through, and then fill in the missing links.

Lovers can write sweet nothings every day, and the missives will be received and treasured. Not so when love begins to die. Now is not the time for writing every day. Used sparingly, letters make a dramatic impact; used too often, they become a nuisance to write and to read.

If you can help it, do not type. There are few things as personal as handwriting. Your mate probably loved your writing when he or she was in love with you, and most probably hasn't received a letter since. Capitalize on the extra impact of a handwritten note. For women only (at the risk of sounding chauvinistic), a little perfume can't hurt.

If you or your mate has a flair for the dramatic, try sending a telegram. "ESSENTIAL THAT YOU NOT LEAVE ME. STOP. WE MUST KEEP OUR MARRIAGE TO-GETHER AT ALL COSTS. STOP. AM SURE THAT WE CAN WORK OUT ALL DIFFICULTIES. STOP. LOVE YOU. STOP." Or, if you choose, send a night letter. A singing telegram is probably a bit too bizarre for most tastes.

Another suggestion: Place an ad in the personals column of the local paper. If you advertise in the paper, though, be discreet. No one wants to be embarrassed in public.

> M.J.
> I love you more than ever,
> I know we can make it work.
> I'm ready to compromise and
> to do what has to be done.
> All my love.
>
> T.J.

Send your mate the clipping. Only the two of you will know. Obviously, it's just a cute trick, but it's one hell of a conversation starter. It will emphasize to him or her that you really care and that you'll stop at nothing to keep the two of you together.

7   Don't Scramble for Moral Superiority

When a good, free-flowing, in-depth dialogue finally begins to unfold between husband and wife, comments are often made that one or the other might take issue with.

"You're inane," he says. "You don't read the newspapers. You embarrass me in front of our friends."

Yow! That hurts. First, because it's not true. You spend a half-hour with the paper every morning in order to be well informed. It's just that you have trouble with the names of all those little countries in the Far and Middle East. And you've never felt comfortable, whether in school or at parties, to put forth your views on current events. And talk about being embarrassed in front of friends! Has he ever heard himself brag about how much money he's got? God! You could die!

Obviously, there are almost *always* two sides to every argument, particularly in a marriage. Take the case of the above couple. It is easy for outsiders to see that neither spouse is blameless. But in this example, the husband is the one who is threatening to leave, and the wife has been trying to convince him to stay by initiating the difficult, often stormy process of dismantling his silence. She has succeeded. He is talking. The only problem is, he is criticizing her, and she feels the stinging injustice of his remarks. Nevertheless, it is sometimes wiser to hear your mate out, calmly and patiently, than to try immediately to rebut his onslaught. Naturally, there is an instinct to marshal a withering counterattack when one's mate begins to attack.

No one likes to be in the wrong. Corporations, governments, guilds, associations, all try to defend or advance their own causes on moral grounds. The need to be "right" seems deeply rooted in human nature. Nevertheless, now may be the time to resist the impulse to prove oneself "nobler" than one's mate. Why can't you be wrong? Or, more importantly, why can't you be right and let your mate *think* you're wrong? It's better just to listen or to respond in such a way that you further draw your mate out. To defend yourself, to prove that it is really your spouse who is in the wrong, may shut him or her up, or may precipitate a hateful, brawling argument. Verbal combat may be better than silence but not nearly so effective as a deep and thorough airing of whatever is on your spouse's mind.

How do you deal with listening to hurtful, possibly erroneous comments about yourself? It's important to remember that these are only words, that the process may actually be a positive one and may bind your mate more closely to you with each new word, although for the moment you may feel the opposite is true. And what good is it to prove to your mate that he or she is at fault if he or she leaves you?

Toward this end, let us examine the case of Robert, a young banker. After several years of marriage and with little explanation, his wife, Evelyn, moved out of their spacious one-bedroom apartment into a studio flat in the arty section of the medium-sized northwestern city in which they lived. Up to that point, their marriage, save for an occasional festive weekend, had not been a particularly happy one. Describing the couple, most casual observers would have agreed that Evelyn was the more physically attractive of the two, while Robert projected an aura that was considerably more commanding, one that gave others a sense of his competence and trustworthiness. With this particular pair, outward appearances were not the least bit deceiving. Evelyn was as cavalier about being places on time, doing the housework, and keeping the checkbook balanced as her casual hairstyle and informal clothing suggested.

Her husband, on the other hand, a man given to traditional pin-striped suits (impeccably pressed and tailored), could not bear to be tardy to a meeting, pay a bill late, or be served by a waiter who was not properly respectful and efficient. All behavior that was not as prompt, orderly, thoughtful, or "correct" as his own made him nervous, even angry. The fact that Robert and Evelyn clashed should not be surprising; it was downright inevitable.

Often she would send in the rent check late or forget to pay it altogether. When the landlord called or sent a note requesting immediate payment of the delinquent sum, Robert would fume. He would also be upset by Evelyn's inability to arrive at social engagements on time, the slovenliness of her corner of the bedroom, and the "inappropriateness" of many of her outfits. One time she arrived forty-five minutes late to meet him at a small dinner party hosted by his boss. The neckline of her gown plunged to her waist. Underneath she was wearing no brassiere, and when she reached forward to pass a dish, Robert could see her entire bosom. He blushed furiously, a mixture of suppressed rage, embarrassment, and jealousy. Surely during the course of the evening others would see what he had just observed. And this was far from an avant-garde crowd. It was not entirely out of the question, in fact, that Evelyn's dress could in some indirect way hinder his career. Suppose several months from now he and a peer at the bank were being considered for a promotion —Willoughby, for example, whose demurely dressed spouse was at this very moment sitting to Mr. Morgan's right, chatting brightly with him about their mutual love of gardening. My God, how could Evelyn do this to him?

Naturally, Robert exploded the instant they got into their car to drive home. She was a flirt, a tramp; she had no conception of decent behavior. She spent too much money in department stores and not enough time cleaning the apartment. She did whatever she pleased without thinking of the consequences to others. In short, he was implying that he was morally superior to her in every way. It was the only response he knew how to make. She had hurt him, had made him feel inferior, unloved, not in control. He wanted to retaliate, to tell her she was not as good as he.

"I'm sorry," said Evelyn. "I had no idea it would be such a stuffy party or that you would get so upset. I really am sorry."

It was not enough for Robert. He continued to reiterate all the nuances of her improper behavior, repeatedly pointing out the things she'd done wrong. Robert justified his words under the guise of helping her see the light so that she could improve herself.

"I'm sorry, Robert. I really am," she replied. "I apologize. I'm sorry. I shouldn't have behaved the way I did. You're absolutely right."

Before they pulled into their parking space, he had extracted over a *dozen* separate "I'm sorry's" out of Evelyn. (Later she would tell a friend, "I have a feeling there's something wrong with my marriage. I always seem to be saying I'm sorry.") Finally mollified, Robert lapsed into his usual silence. Of course he was right. There was something altogether too loose about Evelyn. What she needed was to have a sense of discipline, of propriety.

A psychiatrist could say that Robert's sense of anxiety and frustration was based on more than mere concern for public decorum. He was probably much more afraid that his wife was going to betray him than

embarrass him. Still, others would agree that he did
have a "case": Surely there is nothing particularly
praiseworthy about a mate who is always late, bounces
checks, lets dustballs collect under her bureau, and
leaves her clothes scattered about the room. In a
certain sense, Robert did have a right to feel morally
superior. The only problem is, even though Evelyn
couldn't take issue with his specific complaints, she
really didn't want to change her behavior. Of course,
her husband had been more noble. But he had been
suffocating her from the very start of their relationship,
monitoring how she spent her time and money, and
constantly attempting to shepherd her into a style of
behaving that simply "was not her."

Evelyn was an attractive woman to whom men
responded on sight, a woman with a yen for romance
and fun, whose sense of dignity and decorum was not
really so pronounced as was her husband's. As a
result, what little fun and enjoyment she had gotten out
of her marriage was soon extinguished. Despite the fact
that Robert was "right" and that an impartial judge
might have ruled in his favor, his very need to prove
himself morally superior—with his lectures and denun-
ciations and calls for more dignified behavior—was
what finally drove Evelyn away from him. So what if
he was better than she? He'd become too much of a
prig and a bore and a policeman to provide her with
any of the emotional sustenance she needed. And so,
with little more than a goodbye, she left and moved
across town, into a shabbier building, perhaps, but with
a chance to lead a far happier life.

Thus, for a while, though Robert had proved himself
"better" than Evelyn time and time again, in the long
run he lost a mate. The question we must ask now is:
What could he have done differently to have kept the
relationship together? Or, failing that, what can he now
do to win her back? The answers will be explored
presently. But some of you might be wondering why
we've decided that it's Robert's responsibility to win
Evelyn back. Whoever wronged whom, she is the one

who left, she is the one who had less and ultimately no desire to keep things together.

The sad but undeniable truth is that Robert needed or wanted Evelyn more than she needed or wanted him; one could even say he loved her more than she loved him. Thus, it is he who must make the effort to get her back; it is he who must compromise more. If this reeks a little of "might makes right," so be it. That is often the way life works, in love as well as war.

As difficult as it may be to do, we'd like you now to explore the possibility that it is *you* who is responsible for your mate's dissatisfaction with the relationship. All of us are, of course, much more acutely aware of the faults in others than in ourselves. But now is the time to remove the blinders and take a frank, honest appraisal of yourself, no matter how it may hurt. Have you become too fat, too sloppy, too boring, too quiet, too self-absorbed?

And even if you *are* in the right, why waste time endlessly justifying yourself to yourself? What good is it to prove to yourself that you don't deserve to be mistreated if in fact you *are* being mistreated? Robert was constantly criticizing his wife for her slovenly, inconsiderate, provocative behavior. Yet all his carping and moralizing accomplished was the one result he feared most: losing Evelyn.

What about you?

Are you falling into the same trap, proving to your mate over and over again that you are "better" while at the same time driving him or her further and further away from you?

We have found that the need to be "right" in many people borders on an obsession, so much so that they will cut off their noses to spite their faces . . . or, in this case, win an argument but destroy a marriage. Like most of us, you probably have a sharp eye for picking out your mate's faults, but are you capable of honestly and dispassionately examining your *own* behavior? And can you examine your own behavior without instantly deciding that you're blameless after all? Fi-

nally, are you capable of admitting—horror of horrors
—that sweet, little *you* may actually be the one who
is—dare we write it?—*wrong?*

If you can admit that your behavior may be a
contributory factor in alienating your spouse, in making him or her want to flee, then in our opinion you
stand a far greater chance of holding onto your love
than those who are intent on proving, day after day,
that she's the one who's guilty because she's not
affectionate enough or that he's a beast because he's
always leering at other women. Let's shake things up a
little. Let's scramble our thinking. Let us explore the
notion *So what if my mate is in the wrong?* Rather than
grind his or her nose in that fact, see what other tack
you can take to make your mate love you more, enjoy
you more, enjoy *life* more. This is a path that we, the
authors, believe will yield more positive and healing
results.

To wit, what do you think might have happened if
Robert, the priggish banker, had made an attempt to
cut back on the criticism and had praised his wife for
her attractiveness rather than continually berating her
for her sloppiness and laziness? What if, after the
conservative dinner party at his boss's, he had taken
her to a late-night show or discotheque instead of
having sternly lectured her all the way back to the
apartment?

*But then she might have behaved even more outrageous-
ly,* some of you are probably thinking. *Perhaps she would
have gotten drunk, played footsies with the man at the next
table, discoed right out of her dress and run off with the
drummer.* We doubt it. Giving your mate *more* of what
he or she wants (even if you think it's absurd, immoral,
a waste of time) often brings him or her closer, makes
your spouse feel more affectionate, and breaks down
barriers between the two of you.

Thus, a man who attends the ballet with his wife or a
woman who accompanies her husband to a football
game is someone who obviously has learned the value
of compromise, of yielding, of giving his or her mate

more of what he or she wants. At first, it may feel uncomfortable to indulge your mate in his or her predilections. But when you see what glorious results can ensue, you will soon realize the value of accommodating your spouse. In fact, you may even come to enjoy it.

One last point about scrambling for moral superiority. Try to realize that there are times when even the wisest of us, no matter how passionately convinced we are of our rightness or our virtue, are wrong. One only has to recall the certainty with which humans once believed that the planet was flat, that the sun revolved around the earth, to see that this is so. Yes, you may be right in any given argument with your mate, but how right? 87 percent? 64 percent? 41 percent? Consider that the next time you start clawing your way up Mount Morality. We hope it gives you pause.

8　Changing

"If we don't change, we shall die." This simple phrase expresses a basic principle of biology, a statement about all living things. No plant or animal, no insect or germ, simply *is*. From the beginning of life—indeed, from the moment of conception—to the moment of death, every living creature is in a state of flux.

The institution of marriage has frequently been compared to a living organism: It too must be capable of constant change or it will die. Sitting pat on a good thing simply won't work. If your marriage is completely unaltered ten years from today, it will probably be in big trouble. You may think that you will be the same, but you can be sure that everything else will have changed: your spouse, your children, your parents, your relatives and friends, your work—in a word, the rest of your world.

Change may be good or bad. Frequently, it is both. Having children adds a lot to a marriage but takes away as well. The same is true with being promoted or buying a house or moving to a new city. Even loss and tragedy present opportunities for greater growth and closeness between husband and wife. If we are inflexible, we will spend our days pining away for what used to be. If we can adapt, we will seize the chance to change, and we will grow.

If this were a book about maintaining a good marriage, advice would be a lot simpler. We would tell you to keep your eyes open and to roll with the punches. That advice is too late for you. You've already been punched too hard. Now's the time for catch-up ball: You're going to have to move in double-time to catch up before he or she moves out.

Before we consider some case histories, let us make a few general points about change. Change is threatening to all of us, particularly when we attempt to change ourselves. But there is really no one in the world that you can change *except* yourself. If you can grasp this point, you will be armed with a powerful weapon. Change yourself, and your spouse will be forced to change in reaction to the new you.

We use the phrase "new you" cautiously. We do not believe that any adult can become a "new person." You can't change your personality from A to Z, even if you want to, with the help of the world's best therapist, let alone by yourself. Such a radical personality overhaul is completely unnecessary and sometimes even harmful. In the vast majority of instances, if you change just a little, the effects upon your marriage will be startling.

The notion of marginal change is a powerful one. Let's take an economic example. Say you have four kids, and you are earning $25,000 a year. Hard as you try, you can't seem to reduce your expenses below $26,000, and you keep falling deeper and deeper into debt. Your boss calls you in and, for meritorious service, raises you to $27,000, starting immediately. Suddenly, you're paying your bills and wiping out your loans. That $2,000 raise is less than 10 percent, a marginal difference by anyone's standards. You are certainly not on easy street, but you're no longer lying awake at night worrying about your creditors.

So it is with human change. Your plumber-husband doesn't expect you to learn his trade, but you can find out something about what he is doing so that he can discuss his day with you and feel that you appreciate his work. Your wife of thirteen years doesn't really think she'll find Burt Reynolds if she leaves. She has a right, though, to expect that you'll lose those twenty extra pounds and take her out once in a while.

We do not expect you to do the impossible, only to change in small but significant ways. Some of our suggestions may sound superficial to you, but they will have a major impact on your spouse, far out of proportion to the effort you will have to put out.

Be aware of your behavior. Are you really doing what you want to, or are you locked into a pattern that you can't seem to give up? Do you find yourself acting more and more like your parents, mouthing the words you heard your mother or father say so many years ago? Many of us are compelled to play out scripts our parents wrote, no matter how hard we try to avoid their mistakes. We have seen countless young alcoholics who swore that they would never be like their own alcoholic parents end up just like them. In a similar fashion, a staggering number of divorced young people come from families where the parents have divorced. The point is not to decry your fate and blindly follow it. If you are on a road that seems to be going nowhere, you and only you have the power to change the direction in which you are heading.

A young couple met during their senior year of medical school and quickly fell in love. They found that their backgrounds and values were very similar: Both came from religious immigrant Eastern European families; both grew up in a tradition of sobriety and hard work; both were interested in children, and each had independently planned to have a large family after marriage. It looked to all as if this was going to be a marriage made in heaven.

Stefan, the eldest son in his family, had always planned a career in medicine. His career choice was actively supported by his family, who had gone to no small sacrifice to enable him to pursue his dream. Tanya, the eldest child in her family, had faced a different set of circumstances. Her family was no less loving than Stefan's, and was also inordinately proud of her and of her accomplishments. Yet, for them, it was unheard-of for a girl to go beyond high school, much less to become a physician. Tanya actually shared their Old World values but was still driven forward by her talent and her brains. The family had little choice but to acquiesce. Her mother and father were much relieved when she asked their permission to marry Stefan and not one of those "American play-boys," the family term for her other medical school classmates.

The courtship was a quiet and secure one, and lasted four years until both had completed their residencies in internal medicine. Tanya became pregnant almost immediately after their large church wedding and was quite content to postpone her career until the child was born. But she was again pregnant soon after Anna was delivered, and then again and again and again. Stefan worked hard and spent all his spare time with his rapidly growing family. Tanya would talk tentatively about taking a part-time job at the local medical clinic—a job for which she was considerably overqualified—but she received scant encouragement from her husband. Once again she became pregnant.

After six children and two miscarriages, Tanya was in her mid-forties and had begun her change of life. She again raised the idea of working at the clinic, but Stefan demurred and asked her to wait until all the kids were at least in nursery school . . . and then in kindergarten . . . and so it went. Postponement after postponement, and this professional woman began to wonder if she still had any medical skills left at all. One thing was crystal clear, however: Stefan would never let her go to work! The couple began to argue, the first quarrels they had ever had. No amount of persuasion would work. When he was pinned down at last, Stefan admitted that the women in his family had never worked, and his wife was not about to break the tradition. Tanya had not spent twenty-four years in school to be a housewife, and she threatened to leave. Stefan would not relent, and Tanya left, six children in tow.

Some of you are probably outraged that this woman had sacrificed her career for so long and that her husband continued to act like an A-1 male chauvinist. Many of you might have gotten out of such an arrangement much sooner. But it is not for us to judge the basic values of another couple, particularly if these values are jointly held. Both Stefan and Tanya shared rather inflexible traditional notions, and the idea of a woman's working was difficult for *both* of them to accept. At some point in time, however, the system had to change. That is, unless Tanya planned to go on having babies until she received Social Security. But there came a time when she could no longer harness her considerable energy and talent, just to raising children. Her career, so long put off, simply had to be resumed.

If Stefan had sought our advice, we would have told him that he had to bend. Not a lot. Tanya was not about to become president of the National Organization for Women or the editor of *Ms.* magazine. But she was not about to sit idly at home, either. She needed to change, just a little; and he needed to change with her. As a physician, he should have known that a living organism that cannot bend, ever so slightly, will sooner or later break.

Bobbi and Alan are a much more typical American couple. Bobbi worked as a secretary at a law firm while Alan finished his degree in business. The couple had a sensible two children, and Bobbi stayed home for three years until the kids were out of diapers. Her old employer called one day and offered her the chance to return to the firm to train as a paralegal—a lawyer's assistant. Bobbi bounded at the opportunity. She always loved law but had never thought she would get far beyond being a legal secretary. She could not wait to tell Alan about her good luck.

Alan was shocked. He knew his wife would return to work some day, but not quite yet. He thought that the children should be a little older, and he was more than a bit threatened by Bobbi's working conditions. Visions of flirting attorneys, two-martini lunches, and wealthy and distinguished law clients raced through his head. The thought that his wife would be seduced wasn't Alan's only concern. He was immensely competitive and worried that Bobbi might be too successful in a field uncomfortably close to his own. So while Alan harangued his wife about sexual indiscretions that she had not even contemplated, let alone performed, his real but unadmitted fear was of a power realignment in the marriage.

After a week of battling, both Bobbi and Alan realized that things had to change. What had been a workable relationship during the first years of their marriage and when their children were very small would no longer do. A few years of playing mother was fine, but Bobbi was too intense and ambitious a person to limit her activities to the local school bake sales. In fact, the couple was moving upward rapidly, and Alan recognized that they needed the second income. That second income would also enable him to leave a job he disliked and take a much more satisfying one at a slight cut in salary.

If Alan had been worried about infidelity, he soon realized that there is much more danger from an unhappy housewife making it with the milkman than from a satisfied professional who was strictly business on her job. Alan found it a lot easier than he had feared to adjust to the new sharing of power with his wife. Bobbi had no interest in competing with him. For his part, he immensely enjoyed spending more time with his children and even having some leftover time to spend at the gym.

This story ended happily, but many do not. The key to this success was Alan's realization that he could not prevent change. He might as well have tried to stop the tides. Sure, change is threatening to all of us. But the failure to change holds the real danger. What worked five years ago will not work now. And this young couple can be sure that today's model will not do five years down the road.

Newborns cause major changes in a marriage; so do

children growing up and going to school and becoming
teenagers. A couple must be able to adjust to the death
of parents or the loss of financial security. But just as
challenging is financial success and unaccustomed
wealth. Inflexible marriages can be destroyed by too
much as well as too little.

Has your husband complained to his friends that he
has "outgrown" you? Or your wife to her friends that
you are "not the man she married"? These phrases are
the tipoffs. No one "outgrows" anyone unless the other
fails to change. If indeed you are the man she married,
that may be the problem: You haven't kept up.

It is the rare marriage that has "never" been good.
Any marriage that is worth fighting for must have been
at least adequate in the beginning. At some point in
time, however, one of the partners began to change. Or
external circumstances changed. And the other partner was left behind in a cloud of dust.

If your husband has been telling everyone in town
(except you) how "unbending" you are, then pay heed.
If your wife has been complaining to friends and
relations that "you no longer understand her," beware.
These phrases are the clues that you have not sensed
the changes that have occurred or that you have not
come to grips with them. There are many other key
phrases, too: "he's rigid"; "she seems to be in a rut";
"when we argue, he always says the same thing."

It should be clear by now that change is part and
parcel of every marriage. You may be troubled because
he has grown and you have not. He's been waiting for
you, but you've made no move to catch up. Now he's
about ready to throw in the towel. What can be done?

First of all, be reassured. If you are stuck in a rut,
you've got a problem but not a terminal disease. If you
recognize this fact and admit it to yourself, a small
miracle has just happened. You've begun to change!
It's that simple. You're no longer moaning that things
are not what they used to be. You're now thinking that
you've got to adapt to the way things are.

Maybe you should take off for a weekend with your

closest friend, away from the tension and depression and anger in your home. Then start figuring out what's got to be changed. List the major moves your spouse has made over the last few years and match them with your countermoves. Where has he changed and you kept up or shot ahead? Where have you lagged hopelessly behind? How has your world changed so that neither of you has been able to adapt?

The best way to be objective is to achieve some emotional distance. You will have to adopt a new frame of mind. Pretend for the moment that you are a scientist and your marriage is a laboratory. You have been watching a chemical reaction for two or five or twelve or twenty years. The reaction has suddenly stopped, and chemical A no longer wants to combine with chemical B. Do you get excited? Never. You're a scientist. You take a sheet of paper and you figure out what's going on.

Now, here's a quick course in science for all you nonscience majors. All of science really has just three steps: First, measure and observe; second, figure out what's going on. This is the part where you scratch your head. "Ah hah! I think I see what's happening. And I think I know just what to do to change it." Third, carry out an experiment to see if it does the trick. How do you know? Back to step one. You measure the ways things have changed. If you're happy, fine. If not, you design another experiment.

That's why science works. The scientist keeps an open mind. He believes what he sees, whether he likes it or not. He tries to understand the cause. And then he intervenes to make a change. The intervention is always experimental and not necessarily the final answer. Maybe it will work, and maybe it won't. If not, he'll know to try something else. But the proof is always in the pudding.

George and Dolores had always been a loving couple and were happily married for twenty-two years. On a routine physical examination, the doctors discovered a lump in Dolores's left breast. The biopsy showed a malignant tumor. Dolores underwent a radical mastectomy, followed by months of intensive radiation therapy and drug treatment. Her arm swelled up, she lost weight, and she was frequently tired and cross.

George was a tower of strength. He took care of everything and kept everyone's spirits up. He arranged for the surgeon and the treatments. He maintained a lively banter in the hospital room and kept everyone laughing. When his wife or her mother began to cry, he put a rapid end to that with a witticism or by changing the subject.

He tried to keep the family life as unchanged as possible. He told the children that their mother's condition was "minor," and that everything was going to be "just fine." As the months passed, he continued to spread good cheer and to treat Dolores as if she had recovered from a twenty-four-hour virus. Not that he really expected her to do things she was not capable of doing. He swiftly accomplished the chores himself, and continued to keep things afloat and buoyant.

The couple had always had a full and satisfying sex life, and George expected it to resume after Dolores had been home a month. He made accommodations for her weakness and her pain, of course. But he paid little heed to her depression and her lack of desire. He was already talking about how great it was to "have his old wife home again."

Then, one day, the bubble burst. George came home from work and found a note pinned to the empty chair in which his wife had always sat since her return from the hospital.

Dearest George,
   I am flying to California this evening to live with my sister. I don't know whether I'm coming back. I could not face you to tell you that I can no longer be what you need me to be. I can live with my illness, and I can adjust to my surgery. But you cannot.
   You need me to be well and to be happy, and you

do everything you can to pretend that nothing is wrong. But I am not well, and I am not happy. I'll be all right again, but in my time. Right now, I need only one thing from you: to accept me as I am.

I've changed. That's okay. I'll come home if *you* can change, too.

Dolores

What would we tell George if he came to us? Above all, we would remind him that he cannot change his wife. He can change no one but himself.

First, observe. Dolores has a serious illness. She doesn't talk about it, and you pretend that nothing has happened. You have both been afraid to face reality.

Two, figure it out. Any woman who has lost a breast needs time to grieve. She needs to be able to talk about her loss, and she must have someone to listen to her. She does not want to be told that she is as good as new. She needs to know that she will be accepted as she is.

Three, do something. Tell her that you've let her down. You haven't permitted her to cry for fear of breaking down yourself. Now you're all cried out, and you need her back to help her cry as well. You do not need her as she used to be. You want her as she is.

Let's look at another example. Carl and Allison were a rapidly rising young couple. Carl was doing well at his job as an advertising executive and his wife Allison had become the first woman vice-president of the bank at which she worked.

The couple bought a spacious house in suburban Connecticut and joined the most exclusive club in the area. They always spent a little beyond their means, but so what! There were always Christmas bonuses and those raises that came with predictable frequency.

Then the bottom dropped out. Allison became pregnant and was having a difficult time of it. She had to stop working or risk losing the baby. Almost immediately thereafter, Carl's company declared bankruptcy.

His work had been great, but now he was out of a job.
The bills began to pile up, and swiftly.

Allison saw the handwriting on the wall, but Carl
refused to look. She was not unduly perturbed by it,
either. "Look, Carl. Let's sell the house. It's appreciated a good deal over the last year, and we'll walk away
with a nice bundle. We can quit the club. I'm in no
shape to play tennis, and besides, the Y was always
good enough for me. Let's move back to the Upper
West Side. We'd always lived there, and we were
always happy. We can get rid of both cars. We surely
won't need them in New York."

Carl would not listen. Times were going to get better.
He'd get another job. Allison would be able to return to
work. Maybe they'd win the lottery. They had worked
too hard for their high standard of living, and he was
not about to give it up.

The rest of the story is almost sickeningly predictable. Executive jobs were hard to come by, and Carl
was not about to take anything less than he had been
earning before. Allison grew weaker and weaker
through the pregnancy. She was confined to bed and
finally miscarried. The bill collectors were getting nas-
tier. Allison's parents had never paid a bill late in their
lives, and she could not deal with the angry merchants
and the threatening calls. But most of all, she could no
longer accept Carl's stubborn refusal to see that things
had changed. Finally, one day, she packed up and
moved into her sister's cramped apartment in Queens.

Carl finally got the hint. Within a week, he sold the
house and paid off the debts. He leased an apartment in
New York. He then rented an old hobo suit and came
to Allison's sister's place to reclaim his wife. With
flowers in hand, he kissed his wife and asked her if
she'd come home to their humble flat. Allison was bent
over both crying and laughing at the same time. It was
just fine with her to be a member of the *nouveau poor*.

Carl succeeded in winning Allison back because he
recognized that he had to change. He observed that he
was trying to live like a millionaire on an unemploy-

ment check. He thought about it and realized that people count, not things. And then he acted. He swallowed hard and rid himself of all the things. He changed, so there was nothing left to fight about. Allison really had no choice but to come back.

In every healthy marriage, there are always growth spurts of one partner or another. Maybe you have been so threatened by your partner's rapid growth that you've tried to pull him back instead of waiting it out and then growing yourself. He's angry and resentful. He sees you as a drag. He's been pushing. You've been pulling. Now it's time to cut anchor and start catching up.

Sometimes the growth process is threatening to a couple but in the opposite direction. Your spouse may be disaffected not because you have lagged behind but because you have moved ahead too rapidly. Your mate feels outclassed by you and embarrassed by his or her gnawing feelings of envy. He or she may put down your success, ignore it, become furious, have an affair, and ultimately leave.

Many married people have no difficulty accepting their mates' successes. After all, your financial or personal accomplishments will often bring very real advantages to your partner. Your spouse is more likely to be threatened, however, if he or she is a basically competitive person and views much of life, including marriage, as a contest—in this case, a losing one. Your partner may decide to leave not because of lack of love but because he or she can no longer stand the chronic feelings of inadequacy. Remember the situation at the beginning of *Kramer vs. Kramer*? Mr. Kramer is so involved with his own career, so excited by his own achievements at the ad agency, that he does not discover his wife has been miserable until after she has split.

Competitiveness is a complex issue, and we want to focus here on just one aspect. If your marriage has become unbalanced, if you are moving fast and your mate is standing still, it is critical to recognize what is happening before it is too late. You would be startled to find out how many couples drift apart without either partner, particularly the successful one, realizing exactly what is amiss. It is unlikely that Mrs. Kramer would have gone (and we would have been deprived of a great movie) had Mr. Kramer come home one day and said, "Honey, there's something wrong. I guess I've been so wrapped up in myself that I haven't taken much notice of what's been going on in your life."

If your spouse indicates that he or she feels neglected and chronically frustrated, you may face a tough decision. Will you permit anything, even your marital relationship, to impede your rise to the top? We can only raise the question. Each of you, of course, must answer it for yourself.

More often than not, the dilemma is not so stark. It is rarely necessary to stop flying real airplanes and start flying paper ones just to make your spouse happy. As we have already discussed, a marginal change is usually enough, but now in the opposite direction. Instead of needing to do a little better, you may have to do a little worse. We are sure that these words are an anathema to some; the thought of hobbling yourself in any way is repugnant in this age of individuality and self-actualization. Yet no marriage will work if no one is willing to compromise his or her short-term needs for the welfare of the other. If career means everything, you might be better off finding a good housekeeper and forgetting about mates and children.

Sometimes all that is required is a modicum of sensitivity. Be aware of how you might feel if the shoe were on the other foot. Acknowledge these feelings to your spouse. Be a hero at work, if you must, but drop this act at home. Don't rub your spouse's nose in your success if you think that he or she is feeling competitive or envious.

We know a man who led an exciting and rewarding professional life, and reveled in talking about his accomplishments. At parties, he frequently monopolized the conversation because no one else had stories quite as exciting. Fortunately, he was sensitive enough to recognize that his wife was becoming increasingly distant. When he confronted her, she readily admitted that listening to his adventures made her feel insignificant. She confessed that she had been having an affair with a far less spectacular man but one who did not constantly outshine her. The husband got the hint. He continued to be a dynamo at work but stopped bragging about it at home. He became more interested in what his wife had to say. Her affair faded away, and they remained married.

Success is sometimes relative. In our work-oriented world, closing a big financial deal brings more prestige than planting a vegetable garden. In general, anything that does not earn money or fame tends to be discounted. Yet it often takes as much effort to maintain a home and raise children as to run a business. We would advise the high-flying spouse to pay attention to the quiet accomplishments of his or her more earthbound mate. We would counsel him or her not to put down the other's achievements or to compare them to his or her own. We would advise the hero or heroine to share the spotlight, to take an interest in his or her spouse's writing or singing or sculpting, to acknowledge to the other the value of his or her work.

Strange, isn't it, how human nature works? At the outset of this chapter, we told you that too little growth is bad, and here we tell you that too much can be equally damaging. Actually, there is no contradiction: Any change is threatening, and different rates of growth in a couple are particularly threatening. The basic lesson is to be aware that people don't remain the same forever. You must constantly be on the alert to recognize change before it overwhelms you, and then to adapt to it and turn it to your advantage.

9   Excitement

"Self-destruction" is a popular term these days. A man who has a perfectly good business decides to branch out. Blindly he pours a small fortune into a new enterprise that to his friends and relatives and accountant and lawyer seems fraught with risk. The venture fails. The man loses his entire investment, damaging his sound business in the process. Everyone shakes his head. "Arthur is self-destructive," they conclude.

A woman with a fine family and a loving husband decides she wants more out of life than a career as a housewife. In her teenage years she had been a fine dancer. Now in her mid-thirties she decides that it is not too late to go back and hone her skills and perhaps even win a part in a professional show. She begins practicing two, four, six hours a day, pushing her body and, in the process, her family, to its limits.

After six months she auditions, unsuccessfully, for several musical comedies. Even she is able to see that she is not in the same league as the other aspirants and soon gives up in despair, falling into a long and morbid depression. Her friends cluck knowingly. "Alice should have known she was deluding herself. Why didn't she pick a career in which she had a reasonable chance of succeeding? Whoever thought she was so self-destructive!"

Perhaps her friends are right. And yet, if the need is there, what can the person who is seeking an upheaval in his or her life do to avoid it? Usually, very little, as you've undoubtedly discovered if you've ever tried to talk someone out of doing something that he or she is hellbent on doing. You recite the pitfalls but can see in the listener's eyes that he or she is simply not taking your words in. His or her need to take action, to *do* something, cannot be stopped.

We hesitate to call this almost perverse drive toward chaos self-destructiveness. We all have a need for excitement, and in some people the absolute suppression of this need might prove as injurious as its pursuit.

It is not uncommon in a marriage that one partner has a much greater need for excitement than the other. (Later on we'll discuss the phenomenon of opposites attracting, which accounts for why the highly sexed marry the undersexed, the nervous the calm, and so on and so on.) The question we'd like to put forth now is: Has your mate grown disenchanted with you because you have stifled his or her need for excitement? Think about it.

At a wedding recently, we observed a table of five couples, all married, who seemed to be having a grand time conversing. Several times, however, the band played a particularly lively tune, and four of the couples would invariably pop up and head for the dance floor, one or two of them urging the remaining couple to join in the fun.

"No," the wife would explain. "Harvey won't dance."

"Come on, Harvey," the others would say. "You'll enjoy it."

Harvey would shake his head, resolute in his decision to remain sitting, his wife tapping her feet beneath her chair in time to the music, her eyes staring enviously out at the couples bouncing about on the dance floor.

Surely you have witnessed similar incidents yourself, perhaps even been a participant. The syndrome of the husband or wife who won't dance is almost as common

as a winter head cold, nor do we mean to imply that it is
necessarily any more serious than a head cold. The
husband who refuses to dance may be loving and
supportive, the ideal mate in every other aspect, and
his wife may be quite willing to accept this one little
drawback in their relationship. And yet, in some cases,
the refusal to dance can be a clue, an indicator, of both
a deeper conflict and of problems to come. For if one
mate continually frustrates his or her partner's need
for excitement, the frustrated party may begin to look
outside the marriage to satisfy that need for stimula-
tion.

Now why, we must ask, are the Harveys of the
world so damned intractable about remaining on the
sideline? It's so easy, so harmless, to shuffle around a
dance floor for a few minutes every now and then, to
join a volleyball game at a company picnic, to play
mixed doubles at a tennis party, to indulge one's mate
in his or her craving to go white-water rafting. Even if
Harvey isn't caught up by the spirit of the event, at
least he will be helping his spouse to have a good time.
Where's the harm in that?

Well, there isn't any harm really; in fact our feeling is
that a great deal of good can come of it. The problem is
that Harvey and those like him are sometimes just
plain tired—willing to grow old without a fight. But just
as often they are afraid, fearful that a little dancing will
lead to an orgy, that the physicality and exuberance of
a volleyball game will somehow send his or her mate
flying out of control.

Perhaps you've experienced these kinds of feelings
yourself? A neighbor invites you and your husband to
an evening swimming party to christen their new pool.
The idea of it makes you uncomfortable, and you
decline the invitation, reminding your husband of his
tendency to get ear infections. Your wife proposes that
you join some friends at a jazz club in the city, and you
resist, explaining that jazz clubs are too noisy and
smoky for you.

We'd like to ask you to explore for a moment whether

the avoidance of festive and exciting ventures has become a pattern in your marriage. If it has, you should be aware that you may be suffocating your mate's need for excitement, and this can lead to a problem between the two of you. Perhaps the prospect of spending the next thirty or forty years together without frequenting cocktail lounges, square dances, concerts in the park, without traveling or dining out or even watching an erotic movie on a neighbor's Betamax, does not seem bleak or gloomy to you; to your mate, though, a marriage without these things may seem joyless, hopeless, depressing, and he or she may feel compelled to find excitement outside the marriage.

Our advice is that you head your excitement-seeking spouse off at the pass. As difficult as it may be for you, we urge you to push yourself up out of your seat and accept your wife's request to dance, perhaps even beat her to the punch by asking her to dance first. Get tickets to a play or concert you know your husband would want to see. Make reservations at the new restaurant in town that everyone is talking about. Put together a tennis or swimming or dancing party. Surprise your mate, who is convinced that you are the most reclusive, negative stay-at-home on earth. Incorporate some of the excitement your mate is longing for *into* your marriage right now, today. And calm your fears by realizing that a little excitement goes a long way.

Our experience suggests that many of those who avoid excitement fear that it may lead their mate astray. A wife worries that if her husband sees a pornographic film, it will make him want to have an affair. A husband balks at taking his wife out to a nightclub because he's too tired and convinced he won't enjoy himself. But, actually, the reverse is true. Let a little excitement come into your marriage, and you will discover that not only are you *more* likely to hold onto your mate, but you may very well start having more fun yourself.

Sex, of course, is one of the most obvious arenas of

excitement in a marriage—and also one of the most explosive. In almost all marriages, even in very good ones, it seems that one of the partners feels the other partner is neither interested nor active enough in lovemaking.

The less interested partner tends to view his or her spouse as oversexed. The "oversexed" one sees his or her mate as not loving enough, sexless, too caught up in career, children, or status to take enough time out for him or her. In extreme cases, where lovemaking is infrequent, the deprived husband or wife may walk around chronically angry, sometimes without even realizing why.

Do not think that we are recommending that you use sex as a substitute for good dialogue, for true communication. We have counseled against this throughout the book. At the same time, there are marriages that could be markedly improved if the less active partner would make a greater attempt to provide his or her mate with more sexual excitement. This does not mean that the passive spouse should merely submit more frequently, but rather that he or she should try to be more seductive, more sexual, more of an initiator.

Those spouses who crave increased sexual excitement in their marriage usually want to be met halfway or even more than halfway. They are fed up with always being the one who proposes lovemaking and now need to luxuriate in being the one sought after, the one desired.

Lest such a program overwhelm you, consider that it doesn't take a great deal of sugar to satisfy a yearning for sweets, nor must you stage an orgy to ease your husband's or wife's longing for excitement. In fact, it's astonishing how an occasional bout of unexpected lovemaking, or a night out at a jazz bar, or dinner and wine at a simple, inexpensive restaurant can add romance and change-of-pace to your life together. Even those who fear excitement come to enjoy it when they see it is not dangerous or threatening.

One last point about excitement. Some people have

such a great need for it that they do in fact become self-destructive: the skier who must challenge more and more dangerous slopes, the person who takes up motorcycle racing or skydiving. Some people have such an overwhelming yen for upheaval that there is almost nothing that can dissuade them from the course they have chosen. We have encountered dozens of men and women over the years who have fled from second, third, fourth, and even fifth marriages because they simply could not abide a placid, harmonious, orderly relationship. If you find yourself married to someone like this, you may be wasting your time, energy, money, and health trying to keep your marriage together. Perhaps it is better to start looking for someone to whom you can stay married for a lifetime.

10   When Words Are Not Enough

Maybe one reason we're divorcing so much is we've become too civilized. Too intellectual. Too removed from the basic processes of living.

In the preceding chapters, we've emphasized the importance of dismantling silence, of starting a dialogue and keeping it going. But sometimes talk alone is not enough—you've got to act. In a deteriorating marriage, we often relate to our spouse in a sort of second-hand fashion, as if we were dealing with a problem in logic and not with a human being.

To demonstrate what we mean, let's look at a piece of contemporary life that has nothing to do with divorce: children's play. Not so long ago, we kids played *with* each other. A lot of thinking, and even more talking, went into our games. Rules were agreed on and just as quickly changed. But sooner or later, each of us had to *do* something. When the ball came speeding toward you, all the thoughts and words in the world wouldn't help you knock it out of the park. There were no little buttons to press or digital displays to tell you how you did. It was just you and your bat. You had to take the swing to feel the crash of wood against leather.

You played hide-and-seek by chasing real children. And you played house with real dolls and real dollhouses. Football took strategy, but it also took speed and brawn. There were always rules, but the rules were never fixed.

A lot has changed in the last generation. Kids now play electronically, by remote control. The modern child doesn't need a sandlot. He doesn't need a helmet or a glove or a mask. He doesn't even need other kids.

Want to hit a home run? Five home runs? Easy as pie. No need for the spectacular swing. Just figure out the rules and press the switch.

Basketball? A cinch. Football? Sure. Want a trip into outer space? It's yours for the asking. To make it work, just think it out and push the button. You don't need strength or charm. Save your feelings of elation or defeat. The machine doesn't care. Umpires and referees? Put them in the museum. The machines are absolutely fair. They're clean, automatic, and so, so logical.

Yet for kids, the world has become a passive place. They cannot make the rules, and they cannot change them. They've got to sharpen their thinking skills and even their finger reaction time. But any other action is quite irrelevant. Just think it out, flick your finger, and the deed is done.

Unfortunately, that's not the way it is in human relationships. We have to think and we have to talk, but we've also got to act. Yet so many of us cannot seem to move beyond words. We relate at a distance. When we feel like crying, we talk about how sad we are. When we want to embrace, we express feelings of warm regard. When we want to scream, we go into silent withdrawal.

Let us not paint this trend in purely negative terms. It is truly a mark of civilization that we can solve our differences with words and not with blows. Words themselves can ward off violence and can do much more. For all their power, however, words have their limitations. After an issue is explored and discussed and dissected, there comes a point when one must act.

Ronnie and Cliff were what all their friends would call real civilized people. They were refined and courteous. They never screamed, and they seemed always to be in perfect control. All their friends were shocked when they found out that Ronnie had been having an affair.

Cliff was distraught. He consulted a psychiatrist. He stopped sleeping with his wife even though the escapade had ended as quickly as it had begun. When he felt able to speak to her, he would talk for hours about his wounds.

Ronnie was overwhelmed with guilt. It was a terrible mistake. She assured Cliff that she was no less devoted now than she had been during their fourteen years of marriage. She had been at a librarians' convention, and, well . . . sometimes these things just happen. No excuses. She and Luke had seen each other a few more times over the months, and then both of them had lost interest. That was last year. It would have remained secret forever had Luke's wife not found out and raised a fuss.

Guilt was not good enough. Nor were explanations. It wasn't that Cliff wanted his pound of flesh for the misdeed. He just wanted to explore it. And to dissect it. And to chew it over. And to analyze it. And then to explore it again. Everything else in the marriage was put on hold. The couple knew that the "rational" path was to sleep separately until the matter was ironed out.

After a while the couple was deadlocked. How much can you explore something? Even a major scandal has just so many angles and no more. What of a three-month dalliance between two librarians? Even the town busybody had long since lost interest. Now, we do not downplay the serious implications of any episode of marital infidelity. The point is that there is only so much to discuss.

Ronnie wept softly when she and her husband talked, but did not really cry. Cliff was stern but did not shout. When her husband had had his say, Ronnie felt like embracing him but did not know if he would let her. Between waves of his indignation, Cliff felt tenderness, too, but did not think that these feelings should be expressed.

Ronnie's guilt gradually turned to irritation and then to anger. *Enough, already,* she thought. *It's over and done with. It won't happen again. He keeps digging, but there's really no more there.*

Cliff wanted done with it, too, but he had painted himself into a corner. *Is she truly sorry?* he thought to himself. *Does she love me? Do I love her? What more should we explore?* None of these thoughts was ever verbalized, of course. He wanted his wife so badly that he ached. But neither could break out of the pattern they had imposed.

Throughout the ordeal, Ronnie thought that Cliff would leave. Nothing happened. She became so nervous waiting for the inevitable that she finally decided to bring it about. To get the worst over with. The tension had become unbearable.

"Cliff, this won't work," she said one day. "I take all the blame for what happened, but what's done cannot be undone. I'll leave, and maybe that will help. I want nothing for myself. I'm truly sorry."

Cliff's heart stood still. The drama had played itself out to its logical end. Before, he had lost his wife's fidelity for a few months. Now, he was about to lose her forever. He searched for words, but there were none left. *The words had all been used up.*

And then a sudden inspiration struck him. He reached out and pulled his wife toward him. He held her as he had never held her before. No words were spoken. But both knew in an instant that something amazing had just happened. The spell was broken. They had each other back again.

Magic? Not at all. Just a simple truth about human interaction. People feel what they do, not what they say.

Talk about jumping off the high board all you will.

You won't feel the thrill until after you do it. The same is true of flying or sex or any other palpable human experience. Words are important, but they can bring you only so far down the road. Then you've got to act.

For all the months and months of talk, Ronnie and Cliff could no longer feel or even understand what they were talking about. Sure, the words came out, and they seemed to make sense. But the words were lifeless, manufactured. They were logical enough to anyone who cared to listen. But they had long since ceased to convey meaning.

Concepts like "Do you love me?" or "Can I love her?" became rarefied abstractions, devoid of any significance. Cliff no longer knew if he loved his wife. He could not even tell you what "love" meant.

And then, suddenly, an embrace. Everything was instantly clear. She felt to him like she had always felt: warm and soft and sweet-smelling. Her salty hot tears ran down her face and onto his arm. His body glowed, and he felt a strong stirring in his genitals. Love her? What a ridiculous question. If this isn't love, what is?

The process of psychotherapy is an impressive example of the way that words are used to explore problems. The use of verbal concepts is both the strength and the weakness of the therapeutic experience. At first, we encourage our patients to sit down or lie down and talk. We tell them to censor nothing, to say whatever comes into their minds. Patients learn to explore the unknown, to attempt to fathom the mysterious depths with words.

Experienced psychotherapists recognize, however, that there comes a time when talk should stop and the patient must act. Let's say we are treating a person for his fear of elevators. We can explore the meaning of fear and the meaning of elevators. We can look at his past experiences and his future anxiety.

Sooner or later, though, he's got to take a ride. Only then will he know how it feels. If he does it with ease, the battle is almost won. If his heart pounds and his head reels, at least he's experienced the worst. He's identified the enemy and can begin the conquest. Let him just talk, and he will talk forever.

Sometimes we actually tell patients to stop talking about how they feel and to start acting. "You're terrified of asking women out? You don't think you can assert yourself at work?" we ask. "Do it anyway. We guarantee that the world won't stop. Do it, and we'll talk about your feelings later."

Cliff and Ronnie have showed us that one embrace is worth an hour—or even a year—of talk. That couple's mistake was to talk endlessly. Would they ever embrace again? How would it feel? Would it be right? They thought they had to talk it out before they could act. But they learned (in the nick of time) that it had to be done the other way around. And so they embraced. And then they talked.

Say you and your spouse are caught in a war of words. You're both repeating the same worn-out arguments, and the words have lost all power to persuade. Declare a unilateral cease-fire. "You know, I'm getting weary of all this arguing. There's a great movie playing across town. If we rush, we can just make it, and we can resume our discussion when we get back home."

This kind of approach gets your spouse off the hook when he or she would really like to stop the fight without losing face. It conveys respect for your mate's feelings and permits you to do something together that is enjoyable and nonconflictive. You are not avoiding dialogue. You are merely declaring a rest period after the dialogue has become destructive or after you both have become saturated with words.

Suspending the battle can bring a lot of temporary relief, but sooner or later you've got to stop talking about all the things that are wrong and start doing something to correct them. Timing, of course, is important. But if you wait for the perfect time, chances are you'll never act. You don't need the perfect moment. If you've got a reasonable shot, then take it. Even if you can't find a time that seems right, take it anyway.

Stop talking about what you'll do for her if she stays with you. Do it. Make her life easier. Take her out to dinner twice a week. Show her how to write a good résumé so she can get the job she wants. Embrace her, if she'll let you. If not, hold her hand.

Encourage him to start playing the saxophone again and take the kids away so he'll have time to practice. Take a job if you sense he's weary of being the family's sole support. If he's feeling smothered by family life, send him off on a golf vacation by himself.

Your actions do not have to be heroic, nor do they have to be sexual or intellectual. Expressing your affection and warmth in nonverbal terms, conveying the feeling that this is your spouse's home, and that he or she is cared for and accepted there, may be all that's needed.

Prepare his favorite foods on a regular basis. A heaping portion of homemade crispy fried shrimp can sometimes say more than a heaping portion of words. Give her those total body massages that make her feel she's back in the womb. Within each of us there is a little boy or girl who wants to be taken care of. If you treat your spouse like his loving mommy or daddy once in a while, it will be a lot harder for him or her to run away from home.

Not everything will work, of course, but sooner or later you will find the right combination. And when you do, you might be astonished at the positive effects that can ensue from one tiny action, not just on your mate but on you as well. The very act of doing will change both your attitude and your behavior. Even if you didn't completely believe in your plan at the outset, you'll become a lot more enthusiastic as you put it into action. You'll discover that you begin to feel what you do, not what you say.

Should I start to jog? Will I like it? Can I keep it up? Think about it long enough, and you'll eventually lose interest. Buy a pair of sneakers, though, and you will quickly grow convinced. You'll be sold yourself, and you will soon be selling others on the virtue of the sport. When you were on the sidelines, you were uncommitted and even cynical. Once you began to jog, your very action turned you into a booster for the sport. Doing turns us all into believers.

11   Spending

Money alone will not win back a love. But it surely won't hurt. And we've yet to hear of someone who has been won back by stinginess.

Money is rarely the sole cause of marital breakup. On the other hand, it is the uncommon divorce in which money plays no part. Financial disagreements may have always been a major source of dispute in your marriage. Or, fighting over money may just be one of the manifestations of fighting over everything else. In any event, warring spouses are usually less than generous with one another.

Spend money on that bastard or that bitch? you may be thinking. *You must be crazy. I'm saving my money for the lawyers.* Well, unless you're planning to marry your lawyer, we suggest that your dough had best be spent on your roving mate. After all, you've been saving your stash for a rainy day. You don't need a weatherman to tell you that there's a blizzard out there.

Put very simply, you're in a real crisis, and that's what savings are for. This is the time to pull out all the stops. You wouldn't think twice about dipping into cash to save your house, or your business, or your leg. Just throwing money at these problems won't necessarily solve them. But that won't stop you from trying.

What about your marriage? Money is no guarantee,

but money may give you that added leverage to tip the scales. If you get divorced, it will all go to the lawyers anyway. Or to alimony payments. You might as well invest it in your marriage now, while you still have a marriage.

Now let's get down to how to do it. Rule number one: Spend the money on you and your spouse *personally.* Not on the children. Not on the house. Not into the pension plan.

Rule number two: Spend the money on intangibles, not on *things.* Spend it on travel. On household help. On dinners and vacations. On luxuriant experiences.

Rule number three: If you can't afford it, spend it anyway. If it works, you've gotten more than your money's worth. If it fails? Well, you just won't be able to afford as much alimony as you had planned.

Let's look at a case in point. Ben and Suzanne are in their mid-thirties. They have been married for twelve years and have two school-age daughters. They have always impressed their friends as being the most stable couple around. Friends and relatives were shocked when they heard that Ben and Suzanne were planning to split.

Ben and Suzanne had met in college and quickly fell in love. Their interests were almost identical. The two were especially fond of politics, travel, and disco dancing. They were inseparable during their school years and, to no one's surprise, married right after graduation. They spent a year together in the Peace Corps, which, in retrospect, was the happiest year of both of their lives. They became fluent in Spanish, worked hard, and had a great deal of fun. They were strongly tempted to extend their tour for another year, but Ben was eager to return home and enter graduate school.

Against their better instincts, the couple bought a house in the suburbs. They fell into a lifestyle they had always planned to avoid. Ben commuted to the city, and Suzanne remained at home to care for the two children. Ben was reasonably successful, and there was no real financial need for Suzanne to work. Ben's stance was neutral. Whether Suzanne worked or not was entirely up to her.

The couple took long summer vacations and traveled extensively during the first few years. After the children were born, all that ended. Ben and Suzanne had to come to grips with the realities of home and family. Suzanne wanted to pursue a career after the children were out of diapers, but she seemed to have no direction. She was torn between needing to be a good mother (by the standards of most of her suburban neighbors, anyway) and wanting to do something more with her life.

They stopped traveling. Who can travel with two small kids, a responsible job, and heavy mortgage payments? Ben stopped thinking about politics, and Suzanne's political instincts were all funneled into the local League of Women Voters. Disco dancing? Ben was usually too tired after work to walk the dog around the block.

Ben decided that the family was cramped and that he wanted to enlarge the house. The house was on a nice piece of property, and an addition seemed to make good architectural sense. Suzanne seemed content with the idea, but she was soon seized by doubt and constant worry. The addition would take every penny of their savings just for the down payment. The rest of the financing would come from a second mortgage, which, when added to the rest of the bills, would eat up almost every dollar of the family's income.

The work on the house began and took a lot longer than planned. Suzanne was annoyed at every delay and found herself getting angry with the workmen. She had difficulty sleeping at night. She was irritable even when the laborers weren't around. Ben could not help noticing how his wife seemed to be changing, but he had no success in discovering the reasons why. He tried to come home early so that he could deal with the builders himself, but Suzanne continued to become increasingly morose. The couple stopped sleeping together. Presently, they barely talked. And, just as the work on the house was coming to an end, Suzanne suddenly announced that she was leaving.

Ben was deeply hurt but not totally surprised. He knew that the marriage had been going badly and was almost relieved that matters had come to a head. Now his course was clear. He would drop everything else and figure out what had gone wrong. This was no easy task. Suzanne was a very private person and had not complained to her friends, her parents, or the children. Ben knew he had to go straight to the horse's mouth.

He took an emergency two-week leave from his company and arranged for Suzanne's parents to watch the kids. He bought a two-week excursion to Ecuador, the country where the couple had spent that magical year in the Peace Corps. He asked Suzanne no questions. He told her that he was kidnapping her and that she had better put up no resistance. She didn't.

Before she realized it, Suzanne was on a Pam Am jet with a man she had remembered from many years ago. She began to cry and to talk. The long flight with its splendid isolation (and the ever-helpful flight attendants bearing vodka martinis) quickly undammed the waters. Suzanne talked. And she talked. And she talked.

"I feel like I'm in a time machine. We were here only ten years ago, as free as birds. No jobs. No house. No children. Just us and our ideals and our love.

"Of course, I'm mature enough to know that things change as we get older. I love our children and I love our home. I know, of course, that we're no longer hippies, and you have to work.

"But it seems that everything has gotten out of control. Your work. Schools and driving the kids around to birthday parties. Neighborhood obligations. And the house. Especially the house.

"Even though the addition was your idea, I'll admit I wanted it as much as you. The extra bedroom and the large kitchen were very tempting. But once we were into it, it started to dawn on me what we had done. We had sold the last vestige of our freedom. We had been planning to spend our savings on a hiking trip in Mexico. And we'd have had enough left over to pay for me to return to school.

"But it all went into the house. Every last dollar. I knew that we'd spend the next twenty years paying off the damned mortgage. It felt like a jail sentence. A twenty-year term.

"I know how bitchy I was to the workmen and to everyone else, for that matter. Those unending construction delays weren't their fault, of course. But the sight of them kept rubbing my nose in the fact they were building my prison."

Ben could take a hint. He and his wife were no longer running their lives, their lives were running them. Sure, these material possessions were beautiful. They knew that half the world would give their right arms for the things that they already had. But Ben was not going to make the same mistake that so many others do. He was not about to hold onto his possessions and lose the most important thing in his life.

The journey was a huge success. Not only did Ben and Suzanne relive nostalgic memories, but they were able to recapture control of their lives. When they returned home, they set about unfettering themselves from the tons of possessions that weighed them down. They were not about to become social dropouts. But they knew that there were many options between *la vie bohémienne* and upper-class suburban elegance.

Does this all sound fantastic to you? Taking off from work for two weeks? A trip to Ecuador? Selling your house?

Well, think about it this way. What Ben did not only made sense in terms of saving his marriage, it made financial sense as well. The trip cost a couple of thousand dollars. No small change, to be sure. But really no more than an average retainer to an average divorce attorney. And the house? We can't tell you how many men and women we've seen clutch onto the house in a sinking marriage, only to lose it along with everything else after the smoke had cleared.

Let us then return to the three simple rules for spending money. First, spend it on personal items. Ben and Suzanne moved to a much smaller house in a community a great deal closer to Ben's job. They made a tidy profit on the large house and carried a far smaller mortgage on their new one. Ben saved at least an hour a day in commuting. They took six weeks in Mexico that summer, and were comfortable enough to take the kids along and to teach them Spanish. After the vacation, Ben insisted on daytime babysitters. There was enough money to pay Suzanne's tuition at the School of Visual Arts. There wasn't much left over. They probably could no longer afford a lawyer. Fortunately, they no longer needed one.

Rule number two: Spend the money on experiences, not on things. You've more than likely accumulated enough, and we doubt that lack of possessions is causing your spouse to flee. Spend money on your mate or spend it on the two of you together. Dinners and travel are two obviously good choices. You don't have to be rich. If you and your old man haven't left town for the last five years, a week at the beach would be fine. Or three days on one of those reasonable package deals in the mountains. The two of you used to like lounges? No need for the Ritz. The corner Cozy Inn, on a regular basis, will probably fill the bill if you do it together.

Spend money to get your wife some help around the house. Once again, what you spend will bear some relationship to your assets, your income, and your lifestyle. You don't need to engage a butler and a chauffeur. A cleaning person one half-day every other week will give your wife the message that you care. It will cut a lot more ice than telling her for the five hundredth time that your mother did it without help, so why can't she. It will let her get out of the usual routine, and breathe new life into her and into the marriage.

We are not suggesting that there is any one magic cure. The point is that money can be constructively used to break a logjam, to interrupt a vicious cycle.

He's about to throw in the towel because he comes home dog-tired every night and says he can no longer stand you or the children. Try buying him a membership in the local health club. Or give your neighbor's kid a few bucks to babysit so the two of you can go to the movies every Wednesday night. Or surprise him with a junket to Atlantic City. You may misfire once or twice, but he'll see that you're trying, he'll see that it matters to you.

You can even spend the money on yourself. Develop new interests. Take tennis lessons, for example. Maybe he'll share his favorite sport with you when you show him that you're competent. Enroll in school. Go to the theater with your best friend. Start swimming and exercising. Your spouse cannot but be interested (or at least curious) when you've begun to catch fire.

Now here's an odd thing about human nature. How many people do you know have done precisely the things we've suggested but *after* the divorce? Sometimes it seems like part of the game to go on a crash course in self-improvement after it's all over. Sure it's understandable. Divorced people are depressed. They've been hurt. They want to connect with someone else, and pronto. So they spend huge sums and go through frenetic efforts to shape up and make themselves into more interesting people. Why not do the same things *before* it's all over, at a time when it can do far more good? You'll get a lot more mileage for your money. And you'll be directing your efforts not to a stranger but to your husband or wife.

We think we've made the point that you should invest most of your war chest into personal services or shared experiences and not into things. If there's something left over, of course, a "tangible expression of your esteem" won't hurt. Like a set of gold earrings. Or a watch. Or a cashmere sweater. Or an Atari video game. Presents are always in place, and there are, of course, appropriate gifts for any budget. In our consumer-oriented society, there is no shortage of gift ideas, and we doubt that you need our specific suggestions. One word of advice, though. If you feel that you want to buy something, try to be inventive and romantic. For goodness sake, don't buy her a Mixmaster or a new vacuum cleaner.

The final rule: If you can't afford it, do it anyway. We don't mean, of course, that you should hock yourself to the local mobster. There are some things worse than divorce, like ending up below sea level in a concrete block. If you're a working stiff, a trip to the Riviera may not be in the cards. Besides, you don't even speak French.

You don't have to go crazy, but you do have to stretch. A Big Mac with Cheese is not good enough. Just about anyone can afford occasional dinners in a restaurant. Or a little household help. Or a modest vacation. Or dance lessons. Or a ski trip in February. Or a three-day cruise to Pleasure Island.

Just be warned, Uncle or Aunt Scrooge. This is not the time for stinginess. This is not the time to be penny-wise and pound-foolish. If you're spending a little more than makes you comfortable, you're doing fine. Just think about those hungry lawyers and accountants waiting at the gate for another marriage to bite the dust.

It has been said that money is like a sixth sense, without which one cannot fully enjoy the other five. We know that money cannot substitute for love. But, when used wisely, it can help nurture a fading love back to full brilliance.

Spend Time Alone—Together!

We have just discussed the importance of spending money on shared experiences and only hinted at the need to spend time alone together. Here we're going to spell it out. If the life that surrounds you and your spouse is causing friction between you, then you must isolate yourselves from it, at least periodically. Only then will the tension and rage and blindness that are so often the causes of silence or bickering fall away enough for the two of you to thaw, to unwind, to begin to see in one another the things that attracted you in the first place.

Naturally, you and your mate can't always up and leave for a month at a time. But you can eat dinner without the children. Or eat dinner out. Or spend a quiet weekend in the country together, even if it seems like a dull and joyless notion to you or your mate.

The essential thing, even more important than spending money (and there's precious little of that around these days), is that the two of you spend time together . . . alone. Take a bottle of wine to the park. Go for a long walk around your neighborhood after dinner. Try a lengthy bicycle ride together on a winding country road. Play golf, but only as a twosome. Go fishing on a pond in the middle of the woods. Sit out in the backyard and take in the sun.

Being alone together in these situations will induce conversation, for after a while there is nothing to do but talk. And to start talking and keep talking can be the key ingredient in healing your relationship, as it was with Ben and Suzanne. Don't feel guilty about leaving the kids. Your mission is as important to them as it is to you.

But my mate looks so glum and unenthusiastic when I suggest we spend time alone!

We are quite aware that this may be the case, and we sympathize. We know how painful it can be to realize that merely the *prospect* of being alone and isolated with you is enough to make your mate depressed. And, yet, we maintain that the *reality* of it can be beneficial, that the words and feelings and actions that are evoked when you and your mate interact apart from others are more likely to strengthen than fray the bonds that bind you.

Let us elaborate. One man of our acquaintance, a successful stockbroker in his early forties, tells us that whenever his wife (who he has never felt was particularly worthy of him), announces that she has made plans for them to spend a weekend together at the shore, he is invariably filled with gloom. Instantly an image pops into his mind of his wife and himself driving along a country road with no one else for miles around. The sky is cloudy, his face is grim, the car is silent, and the chance for fun or romance or joyous sex seems woefully remote.

And yet, he admits, not long after they set off on one of their weekend jaunts, a curious process begins. He starts to relax. He forgets about the stock market, his aggressive, competitive, high-powered colleagues, and the pressure-packed pace of his business life in the city.

All of a sudden his wife no longer seems so naïve or childish to him. Feelings of affection and warmth begin to mount in his chest. The sexy, competent aura of the well-tailored women brokers in his firm starts to fade— in fact, it seems rather brassy and cold when compared to this accepting, loving woman sitting beside him. She looks a bit prettier than he recalled, more a complete person than she seemed just a few hours before. It strikes him as impressive that she has engineered this trip all by herself, mapped out a route and an itinerary, made reservations in restaurants and hotels hundreds of miles from their home. And as they spend time together, they begin to talk and to exchange feelings and thoughts about the children, their relationship, life in general. By the time they return home, he confides, he is deeply in love with his wife again. Of course, it rarely takes more than a few weeks before some of his antagonistic feelings toward her return. But knowing that they are not necessarily permanent takes some of the sting out of them. And he has come to learn that they can be made to disappear entirely if he and his wife set off on one of their mini-vacations again.

There are several lessons that can be drawn from this case. First, once a hostile husband or wife realizes that hateful feelings do not have to be permanent, he or she may not find them so threatening to the marriage, if and when they return. He or she will understand that, like most feelings, they ebb and flow.

Even more important, it can be misleading to assume

that your mate's hateful feelings toward you have anything to do with *you*. Often, stress caused by children or work provokes people to behave offensively toward their mates. Remove the stress, and soon thereafter you may see the sneering, negative behavior disappear.

To understand this, it is useful to be familiar with "displacement" and "projection," two fundamental psychological processes through which people attempt to protect themselves from being hurt.

"Displacement," for example, means that your wife redirects her anger from its appropriate target to someone or something else. She does this because it is too dangerous to attack the real source of her rage. Her boss yells at her, so she kicks the dog or screams at the kids or complains about the way you dress. It's not very noble, but it's a lot safer for her to yell at someone or something other than her boss.

It is difficult for people to acknowledge that they are displacing feelings because most of the time they are not aware they are doing it. Like all psychological defense mechanisms, displacement is largely an unconscious process. You will never get your mate to admit that she's taking her frustration out on you if you confront her head-on, right in the very midst of her frustration. Just being alone together, though, far from the stresses of everyday life, makes it a lot easier for her to see who is truly giving her a bad time and who is her real friend.

"Projection" is a somewhat subtler defense. Your husband is feeling rotten about himself. A colleague got a promotion and he didn't. His ego is at rock bottom. He is depressed as hell. Yet it is too painful for him to recognize the real source of his self-loathing—himself. As a slide projector casts an image onto a screen, he projects his deep negative feelings onto everyone around him, especially you. *My wife is a dullard. She's unattractive. She's got no self-respect.*

And then he gets angry when he starts believing his own projections. *How unfair. I'm so great and I have to put up with this unappreciative nobody. Why do I have to tolerate a fool like her?* And on and on. If your husband thinks like this for a while, he will blissfully forget that it is he who is really down on himself. He will think instead that everyone else is destroying his life, and he will react in anger.

Projection is usually a knottier problem than displacement, because self-loathing is a vicious cycle. Yet if you and your mate summon the courage to head off into the country together, the cycle can be broken. Your husband will experience a diminution in feelings of anger and dislike toward himself, and a rise in self-esteem and self-love. He will start to project positive feelings onto you in place of negative ones, and it will then become easier for him to enjoy and love you.

Thus, if your mate is acting toward you in a way that is suffocatingly hostile or bleakly silent, and you fear that it bodes poorly for the future of your relationship, we suggest that spending low-key periods of time alone together, away from the company of others, may be an effective way to relieve the pressure. And when that happens, the two of you will more readily strengthen the positive, loving ties that make a marriage more secure.

12   Sharing the Burden

We've just examined how the creative use of time and money can help revive a failing marriage. But what if there's not even money for the basics, let alone the extras? What if you are having trouble setting the table or paying the rent, and your spouse says that he or she has had it and has decided to walk out?

We recognize that some couples are really economically pressed, and their financial embarrassment may be the major cause of their marital embarrassment. Money problems can come from being born poor. Or from being sick. Or from being out of work and out of luck. Or from being just plain lazy.

On the other hand, poverty alone will rarely destroy a marriage. To be sure, economic hardship is a major stress, particularly if it is sudden and unaccustomed. Yet most marriages can tolerate financial problems if, and only if, both partners are willing to play fairly. If your spouse begins to feel that you're having all the fun and he or she is doing all the work, you're in for big trouble.

Bluntly put, marriage is in large part an economic venture. Throughout history, the essentially practical nature of marriage was acknowledged by everyone. Marriages were arranged for financial convenience (and still are today in less affluent parts of the world). No bones were made about the importance of a bride's dowry or her bridegroom's inheritance. Each recognized his or her dependence on the other to run the home or the farm. Whether they liked children or not, the couple bore lots of kids out of sheer necessity. Offspring were essential additions to the family work force.

Nowadays, we like to think we marry for love. And for sex. And for emotional fulfillment. To a large extent, of course, we do. Most of us want more from a spouse than a good worker. Yet, when the glow of the honeymoon dims, all couples come to see that, love or not, marriage is very much a business partnership.

Sounds cynical? Not at all. Despite our society's prosperity, in many ways it is harder than ever to make ends meet. There's no more family farm, and children are no longer a source of free labor. They may be lovable, but let's face it: You can't look to kids for help in supporting the family or in making it run.

Gone, too, are the extended families, where the whole team pulled the burden together. Marriage today has become a two-horse dray. Young children, old parents, possessions, and property are all dead weight. There is no one to do the pulling but you and your spouse.

Suppose you decide that it's your turn for a free ride. Forget it. That will leave just one horse pulling the load, and that nag won't be willing to do it alone forever. The harness will quickly begin to chafe. He or she will soon be dreaming of greener pastures.

Let's consider the case of Calvin and Marian. These two young people, who had known each other virtually all their lives, grew up in a small southern town. Both were raised by hard-working and hard-drinking mothers. Both had fathers who had left many years before.

The two first dated in high school. Calvin was a junior, and Marian had just started. They soon began to sleep together, and both discovered that the world held greater thrills than algebra and English composition. Calvin left school at age sixteen to take what seemed like a good-paying job in a warehouse. He wanted a car and an apartment—and, most of all, he wanted Marian as his wife.

Though dismayed at his dropping out of school, Marian was impressed by her boyfriend's industriousness. Calvin was generous, too, and spent all his pay on things that the two of them could enjoy. Marian liked those little luxuries of life that neither of them had known as children. When Calvin asked her to marry him, she quickly accepted.

The couple did well for a while. They rented their own place and began to talk about having kids. Calvin routinely gave his paycheck to his wife, and he seemed quite modest in his personal needs. Marian became pregnant as soon as she graduated from high school. Little Cal was born, and Calvin was immensely proud.

Calvin and Marian had always enjoyed sex with each other, and Calvin now seemed to want it every day. Marian was usually game. Even if she was overtired from work and from being pregnant, she never refused him. "A man has a right to expect it from his wife," she would say. "It's a woman's job to satisfy her man."

A few months after she gave birth, Marian took a job as a secretary in the local textile mill. She advanced rapidly and soon became executive secretary to the vice-president. She was now earning more than Calvin. Calvin began to drink a little too much. One day he quit work in a huff. A few more brief jobs followed, but Calvin was soon staying home most of the time and collecting unemployment.

The couple began to quarrel. Calvin refused to help around the house. He refused to change diapers or to do anything else he considered "woman's work." To make the point, he strewed his own clothes around the floor. He claimed that his male pride had been wounded by Marian's better-paying job, and then by his being fired by his last boss. He had never done housework before, and he had no intention of starting now. One more blow to his masculinity was too much.

For her part, Marian didn't expect Calvin to wash the dishes or feed the baby. She was actually as traditional as he, and equality of the sexes was the furthest thing from her mind. But to her way of thinking, the traditional male role didn't include lying around the house and sipping beer. A man who did not work was simply not a man.

Calvin started to drive a cab because driving permitted him to work when he felt like it. He made a good start, but, as time went on, he seemed to feel like it less and less. The little money he made went mostly for drink and for fancy clothes. If Marian complained, Calvin insisted that he was working and that he did not have to account to her for his hours. They continued to argue about money. When Marian turned up the pressure, Calvin drove a little more. When her attention was distracted, the hack stayed at the garage.

After three years of this, Marian decided to call it quits. Calvin was a little too high to see the tears in her eyes the night before she left. The two made passionate love. ("Why not?" Marian would later say. "Sex had never been a problem.")

When Calvin discovered the next day that his wife and child had left, he was more puzzled than angry. He called Marian at her mother's house.

"Why?" he asked.

"Because you're no man," she replied.

"You're nuts," he screamed. "Who else could satisfy you like I did last night?"

"No one said you're not a stud," she said sadly. "But you're not a man. And I need a man, not a stud."

The couple moved back together and tried to make it work a few more times, but it was quite pointless. Calvin had absolutely no idea what his wife was talking about. He was in his mid-twenties and was a strapping, handsome fellow. All his other women friends thought he was a man. His mother thought he was a man. He remained puzzled. And he remained out of work.

Calvin and Marian ultimately separated for good. They often saw each other around town, and they enjoyed each other's company, as they always had. Marian refused to sleep with her husband, but they occasionally went to the movies together (Dutch treat). Calvin spent a good deal of time with his son, playing baseball and soccer and taking him for rides. When Little Cal was sick or when he needed some new clothes, however, his dad was nowhere to be found.

Marian finally filed for divorce, and though Calvin didn't want it, he put up no objection. The court ordered him to pay a small amount of alimony and child support. He wasn't angry. He just never paid. Marian noted wryly that the divorce decree was worth no more than the marriage certificate.

We spoke to Marian at length. We asked her what made her leave a man she was obviously still fond of.

"I was tired of supporting him. He never tried to get his act together. He just blamed me for all his faults. He called me a domineering woman. But I was always submissive to him and tried to take care of his needs. He didn't know a good thing when he had it. Now the well's just dried up."

We asked what Calvin could have done to keep her home.

"Just go to work and keep a steady job" was the simple reply.

"What about his drinking? And his running around? And his refusal to help you with the household chores?" we asked.

Marian shrugged, somewhat bemused by our middle-class mentality.

"Oh, men drink and they run around. They always come home. I don't expect a man to be changing messy diapers. But Calvin's no man. He doesn't work. A man that doesn't work is no man."

The issue here is really not one of philosophy. Marian and Calvin came from similar backgrounds and, in fact, shared an almost identical set of values. It was not that the rules of the game were in question. It was just that Calvin didn't play by those rules. He wanted to have his cake and eat it, too. He refused to do his fair share.

Doing your share in a marriage is often seen in economic terms, namely, earning a living. Unfortunately, this frequently becomes a male-female issue. In today's world, though, breadwinning is no longer a male monopoly. The curse of Adam is now also the curse of Eve. House-husbands and working wives, though still the exception, are no longer rare. Much more common, however, is the modern marriage in which both partners, like it or not, work outside the home. But doing your share means more than bringing home the bacon. It means taking your fair half of the bad as well as the good.

You may have heard the story of the proud mother and her two recently married children. "How's your daughter doing?" asks the woman's friend.

"Wonderful," she replies. "She married this terrific man who waits on her hand and foot. She likes to sleep late, and he brings her breakfast in bed on his way to work. She can lounge around all day if she wants to. He's sure to come home every night with chocolates and flowers."

"And how about your son?" asks her friend.

"Terrible," responds the woman. "He married this lazy woman who demands that he wait on her hand and foot. She always sleeps late, and she expects him to bring her breakfast in bed. She likes to lounge the day away. And every night she wants my son to bring her chocolates and flowers."

It's human nature to see things from our own perspective, genuinely to believe that we're doing more than we really are. You might, in fact, have started out shouldering equal shares. But balances in a marriage tend to shift over time. Now your wife feels that you're not doing all you can to bring home a good salary. Or your husband thinks that you've become a spoiled princess.

Imbalances of this sort breed chronic, smoldering

resentment and the feeling of being used. The cure is actually quite simple. It's called rebalancing the scales. You've got to let your spouse know that you are prepared to accept your fair share of the burden.

First, you must be able to admit that you've been wrong, that you now realize that you can do better. When you first married, you and he used to go to work together, and you shared everything. A few years later, you cared for three small children while he worked hard to bring in the money.

But the kids are now in school, and you've made no attempt to go back to work. He's holding down two jobs, and he's really breaking his back. If you're honest with yourself, you'll admit that you're no longer holding up your end. Perhaps you can understand why he's become bitterly resentful of your daily tennis lessons and your weekly exercise salon.

Second, talk it out. Once you're ready to acknowledge that the balance in your marriage has shifted, perhaps unfairly, you'll be better prepared to tolerate your spouse's rage. Maybe he or she is justified. Your wife has had it with going to school and working and caring for the children. She doesn't think you're overstraining yourself doing freelance writing. She doesn't want to crush your creative spirit, but you haven't sold a story in a year. What's worse, you haven't really tried.

Perhaps you need to hustle more. We know you would rather write than sell. But unless you start to pound the pavement and to push your work, you'll probably remain an undiscovered genius. Maybe you should take a part-time job. You've done construction work before, and you know you're strong enough to do it now. Artists have labored since the beginning of time to support their families and their art. But whatever you choose to do, don't just sit there waiting for the muse while your wife is over her head in rumpled clothes and dirty dishes.

Suppose you are a housewife and your calendar is filled with leisure activities. Perhaps the suburban life has made you soft. Try chucking the facials and the mah-jongg. You, too, could take a part-time job. If that's not in the cards, perhaps you'd best devote your spare time to your husband's personal comfort or his financial success. Straighten up the house, the way he likes it. Cook those special meals. Keep the kids quiet so that he can nap in peace. Rub his back. Offer to entertain his boring business friends. Don't giggle over mindless sitcoms while he struggles over the work he's brought home from the office.

Third, put your money where your mouth is. Do what you say you're going to do. Do it after you talk it out, or do it right off to show him or her that you mean business. But don't build up your partner's expectations and then fall down on the job.

What you do may seem insignificant, but it can make all the difference between your mate's taking off or giving it another try. He's a highly paid electrician. What can you earn helping at the candy store? She's making a nice income as a teacher. Why should you work a few extra hours at the plant?

In this day and age, unless we're wealthy, every little bit helps. But even more important, pitching in shows that you care, that you understand your mate's frustration and are willing to roll up your sleeves to help out, that you see your partner is going under and are willing to do something about it.

It shows that you are prepared to compromise. That you are prepared to be unselfish. That you are prepared to do almost anything to win her back or bring him home.

Offer to Take Over

Sometimes in a troubled marriage you may temporarily have to do more than your fair share—sometimes far more than your fair share. Why? Because you may discover in the process of dismantling your mate's stony silence that the source of his or her discontent is *self*-loathing—not hatred of or dissatisfaction with *you*.

She feels unattractive because she is getting older. He cannot abide the loss of his hair. She is getting nowhere in her job. Despite success in his career, he suddenly feels his life is meaningless.

Let your mate get all his feelings out. Don't cut him off at the pass, but don't leave him stranded either. Once he's unburdened himself, it's your turn to act. Promise to be there for your spouse, to be supportive, to help him find his way, to be a partner in his woe, to take over responsibility for his life, even as a parent does for a child.

If you are a particularly competent person, offering to take over may be your strong suit. Our experience has been that people often turn to others *outside* their marriage when they have an inner feeling that their life is in shambles, that they cannot go on, that nothing will save them. We've seen men and women initiate self-destructive affairs that have ultimately led to the break-up of their marriage because they've been faced with seemingly insurmountable business or tax or health or career problems.

Take the case of Tom and Sally, a couple who lived in a large northwestern city. Tom ran a successful family shirt company. Until recently, business was good and the couple always had plenty of money. They were able to dress, entertain, travel, and dine out lavishly. Several years ago, however, the business slumped, and it became more and more difficult for Tom to finance the grand lifestyle to which he and Sally had become so happily accustomed. Still, they persisted in spending freely. It was too difficult to break old habits, too embarrassing to admit to their friends that they needed to economize.

Perhaps the business could have survived had Tom and Sally not taxed it so heavily with their constant need for more cash. But before long, it was faced with bankruptcy. Around the house Tom became grimmer and more silent. Sally sensed something was wrong, but every time she tried to broach the subject of how the business was doing, Tom would fly into a rage and tell her to leave him alone, that everything was going to be fine. She did not persist, half out of discomfort in the face of his anger, half out of fear that he might really tell her what was wrong. Like most of us, she enjoyed neither bad news nor the prospect of a lower standard of living. And so they continued in their ways, eating at the best restaurants in town and buying new cars and clothes as if business were booming. With their friends Tom was gay and manic, drinking heavily, laughing heartily, telling stories with flair and drama. At home, he became increasingly quiet and withdrawn. And then one evening after dinner, he simply announced to Sally that he loathed her, was repulsed by her, in fact, and was leaving. He stood up, packed his bags, and moved in with a woman who designed shirts for the business. A few months later he declared bankruptcy.

The aftermath of their breakup is this: Sally has had to go back to work to support the three children; they live a hand-to-mouth sort of existence. Tom has drifted toward New York, claiming that he is trying to find himself, something he has never had the chance to do, what with having been whisked into the family business immediately upon graduation from college.

Now we must ask: Is there anything Sally could have done to have held onto her husband and family, and prevented their lives from flying apart? Our answer is a qualified yes—qualified because it is easy to be clever and glib with hindsight, and one never can be certain how any particular initiative would have worked when applied to real life. Nevertheless, we would have offered the following prescription, for it is our experience that such a program at least stands a *chance* of working, and we think almost anything is worth trying if it can help keep a viable marriage together.

We think it was Sally who had to act because Tom had reached the stage where he was beyond caring. She should have offered—no, *insisted*—that Tom let her help solve his business problems. Sally was a competent woman, the mother of three children, a homemaker who hired plumbers, tree surgeons, gardeners, dry cleaners, roof repairers. She attacked her household chores with efficiency, pride, perfectionism. And she might have had equal success in working with her husband's accountant or lawyer or sales manager or some combination thereof, and together they might have managed to keep the business afloat. Certainly, women have taken over their husband's businesses before and have run them profitably—sometimes far better than they were being run in the first place. It is entirely possible that Sally could have done the same while working out a more economy-minded budget for the family to live on as well. Perhaps this would have given Tom enough time to recuperate and have kept him from bolting out of desperation.

Granted, it may not seem like an attractive notion, particularly to the more conventionally minded, to think of a husband collapsing, giving up, turning over all his problems to his wife. How unmasculine and infantile! And yet, if it works . . . well, then, really what is so bad about it? Don't we all have the right to break down once in a while?

When you come right down to it, all of us have unconscious dependency feelings, the wish to be taken care of by others from time to time. In our sex-role stereotyped society, women are allowed to express these feelings of dependency, but for men they are taboo. The converse is true as well. Men are trained as small boys to express their assertiveness and ability. Equally competent women are taught that boldness is an unfeminine trait.

This is why it is so difficult, in the case we have just seen, for Tom to admit that he's hurting and for Sally to take control. One of the signs of a well-adjusted man or woman, however, is the flexibility to operate beyond the confines of sex-role stereotypes. A man should have available to him both the dependent and the aggressive option, and a woman should be able to be either bold or gentle, as the circumstances dictate. In the case at hand, Sally would have done well to have acted assertively, all the shibboleths about femininity be damned.

Let us summarize by suggesting that if you feel your marriage is being threatened by a mate who feels that he or she is overwhelmed by problems too embarrassing to reveal, a mate who is looking to escape his or her present situation because he or she feels overwhelmed, perhaps it is time for you to suggest gently that you are willing to help, to take over if need be. Like a loving parent, your words may be sheer manna to your tortured mate's soul. He or she may open up to you as never before—and isn't the airing of a problem often the beginning of its resolution?

Are you competent? Strong? Willing to wade head-on into the heart of a thicket of problems? Then perhaps taking over is the perfect answer to your troubled marriage. Think about it.

13   Your One Great Strength

It has been our experience that people who are struggling to hold onto a mate feel an enormous sense of impotence, powerlessness. And that is why it is so important not to lose sight of the fact that you have one great strength on your side that perhaps you are not aware of, that you may even consider a weakness. Yet it is an asset that can do more to keep your marriage whole than your intelligence and your looks and all your skills and talents combined: *That strength is your love for your mate.*

He or she knows this instinctively. Others may like your mate, be charmed by, attracted to, even willing to sleep and marry and have children with him or her. But there are few others, if any, who will love your spouse; and probably no one who can love him or her as deeply as you.

Let your mate know this often—in word, in writing, through your gaze and touch, not pathetically or weepily but openly and graciously. It will make your spouse extremely fearful about ever losing you.

To be truly loved is something people are loathe to give up, for it reawakens in them the feeling of what it was like to be loved as an infant, unconditionally, adoringly. In fact, there is a great deal of evidence that the reason we are drawn to one person over dozens of others is an unconscious realization that he or she is the only one whose love for us can approximate the parental love we received as a child. An alienated spouse may have drawn up a long list of logical reasons why he or she wants to leave you, but these can be erased in an instant by the lonely image of what it would be like to live cut off from your special love forever.

How can you communicate to your husband or wife the intensity and uniqueness of your love? Perhaps the following scenario will be of help.

Picture a couple in their mid-thirties driving home from a party. Helena, a slim, attractive woman with raven hair, is wearing a tight, revealing dress. Her husband, Sal, has also attempted to create an aura that is sexy and appealing, but he is a stout man with a weak chin and a bald spot emerging at the crown of his head. His face is warm and kindly, but the truth is, his overall appearance lacks the obvious appeal and sensuality possessed by his wife's.

As they return home from their evening out, Helena is staring out the window, away from her husband, who is piloting the car. He glances over at her, but if she notices at all, she seems intent upon pretending she doesn't. Sal clears his throat. "You looked very pretty tonight."

Helena mumbles her thanks.

"That's one of the things that makes me love you so much . . . your prettiness."

Helena flashes him a brief smile, but it is clear that she is resolved to keep a barrier between them, to keep Sal from chipping away at her wall of coldness and aloofness.

"Other people noticed, too," he says. "Jim couldn't keep his eyes off you . . . his hands, either."

Helena doesn't say anything.

"You seemed to be enjoying it as well," he adds. "It hurt my feelings."

"Oh, don't be ridiculous," snaps Helena. "It was just a little harmless flirting."

"I don't know about harmless. It seems every time we go out these days, Jim is right there, cornering you, dancing with you, patting your backside, hugging and kissing you at the slightest excuse."

"So? It's fun being paid attention to by other men."

"I'm sure it is. The only problem is, it's starting to seem excessive. And the one man at the party who is absolutely berserk about you, who really and truly loves you—me, your husband—is made uncomfortable by it."

"Alright, already! You're suffocating me with this love. I'm an attractive woman, Sal. Men look at me. They want to go out with me. And I want to go out with them, too. Being married to you just isn't any fun anymore."

Sal shrugs, a trifle sadly. "I'm sorry to hear that. To think that it's so important for you to be admired by other men is painful to me. I wish that you could be as satisfied being married to me as I am being married to you."

"I'm sorry, Sal. I can't."

"I guess that's the way it'll have to be then. I just want you to know, though, that while others may be attracted to you, I'm the one who loves you. I've loved you when you were sick, I've loved you when you were down, and I'm prepared to love you for the rest of our lives, come what may."

Perhaps there are those of you reading this who are wondering why we aren't recommending a more aggressive, combative tack, something on the order of, "I forbid you ever to so much as look at Jim again!" The answer is that this book is aimed at people who lack leverage in their marital relationship. It is not advisable to deliver ultimatums unless one is fully prepared to act upon them. Had he forbade Helena to converse with Jim, Sal would only have been inviting her to defy him. And had she defied him, his only alternatives would have been to leave (which he doesn't want to do) or stay and have his wife realize that his threats are idle. On the other hand, were he to say nothing, to remain silent, he would have been condoning his wife's overtly flirtatious behavior. And to those of you who counter, "*My* mate can see my disapproval just by reading my eyes," we reply, "How do you know for sure?" Unless a feeling is expressed verbally, emphatically, repeatedly, it may be ignored or overlooked, no matter how certain you are it is being taken in.

Sal chose a wise middle ground. Without outrightly threatening her, he was letting his wife know that she was gambling with something she was probably not prepared to lose: the security of his love. Of all our deepest fears, the fear of abandonment may be the most terrifying. Yet abandonment is a double-edged sword; it often cuts the one who leaves even more than the one who is left. Think of all the leavers you know who ask (or would like to ask) to be taken back.

If it is your feeling that your mate is growing apart from you, remind her that there are a lot of selfish people in the world. While others may be seeking a sexual liaison, it is you who really *loves* her. She will not take this lightly. To tell her that you are the one person in the world who loves her *most* is mind-opening. As cavalier as many of us have grown about the sanctity of relationships, the knowledge that one is loved and that one will always have a warm, accepting person to come home to, no matter how sour one's luck and life might have turned, is a powerful magnet, a soothing tonic to the insecure, tormented soul that resides in everyone.

Thus, if you really do love someone powerfully, completely, more than anyone else in the world possibly could, try to see this as a strength rather than a weakness, for the truth is, in the long-run, it may be far more of a factor in binding your spouse to you than your looks, wit, charm, intelligence, or any of the other traits normally associated with attracting the opposite sex.

For most of us, our first relationships in life were with our mother and then our father, who more than likely loved us as an infant with an openness and an acceptance that we generally try to replicate with another when we reach adulthood. On at least one level, your mate selected you because you made him feel loved in the same way his mother or father did. There may be very few others, if any, out there in singlesland who can do the same for your spouse.

Express Your Love Freely and Fearlessly

This is a culture in which it is often considered weak and pathetic to admit one's feelings of love for and dependency upon another. And so instead of showering our mate with comments like "You mean so much to me," or "Just being near you makes me happy," or "I never thought I could love anyone as much as I love you," we suppress the impulse to speak aloud our affection for our husbands and wives, leaving them but to guess at the intensity of our emotions. During times of stress in a relationship, when one or the other party feels he or she is being abandoned, the instinct to clam up is even greater. One fears appearing doubly pathetic: left and still in love.

Yet it is often the opposite that proves true. Those who have discovered how to push through their timidity to verbalize their feelings of warmth and affection tend to *keep* their lover, while those who are unable to communicate their loving feelings are more likely to lose theirs. Let us examine why.

First, consider what happens when you *refrain* from telling your mate that you love him. While you may assume that he can't help but know—such is the intensity of your feelings—the reality is that unless someone is clearly and specifically informed about the way you feel, he can make only an educated guess about what lies in your heart. We often hear husbands and wives declare that they have grown so close over the years that they have only to look at one another to know what the other is thinking. This may be true about the thoughts they are harboring about their neighbor's new puce-colored station wagon, but we do not accept the reliability of the nonverbal approach when it comes to conveying loving feelings. People don't know unless they are told. And if they are not told that they are loved, they are more likely to stray, to take their relationship less seriously, to use their sense of being unloved as a rationale for seeking out love from others.

Ann and Barry are a case in point. In the midseventies, Barry, a slim, handsome man with red hair, was a young accountant in a large firm, earning little money in a grueling, far from glamorous job. Ann, on the other hand, was an assistant TV producer for a daytime quiz show. For someone of her youth, her salary was high, her expense account liberal, her job milieu exciting, both to herself and her friends. There was a sensuous quality to her appearance, abetted by too fleshy lips, a large bosom, and dark curly hair. But her features were not fine, and she weighed ten or fifteen pounds more than she wanted.

Barry and Ann met at a crowded apartment party in an Upper East Side Manhattan high-rise, where neither of them knew the host. Someone dropped a contact lens, and they quite naturally fell into conversation as they searched for it in the shag rug. Later, they went out for a cup of coffee and exchanged telephone numbers.

Several weeks later Ann called Barry to see if he would accompany her to the theater. Her boss had given her two free tickets to what was then one of the most popular shows on Broadway. After the performance, the young couple had dinner and a bottle of wine. Her tongue loosened, Ann spoke with great animation about her ambitions. One day she would like to be producing shows wholly on her own. Barry listened raptly, his eyes shining with admiration. When he brought Ann home, she invited him in. And there began a four-year courtship that was to be marked by both tension and affection.

Barry seemed the more eager of the two to get engaged. Ann fended him off, saying she felt she was too young to settle down with just one person. She insisted they date others, play the field, sow their wild oats. Barry complied but only out of self-defense. His deeper impulse was to marry, settle down, have a family. He asked Ann to move in with him. She refused. She sensed there would be no escape. There were too many handsome, dynamic men at the network who asked her out, away for weekends in the Berkshires, the Hamptons, even California. She did not want to give all that up. True, Barry was sweet and loyal and giving. But would she grow bored with him? And how did she know that one day in the future he might not develop *wanderlust* himself, what with his trim good looks and his magnificent mop of red hair?

After several years of dating one another, Barry's and Ann's relationship developed a kind of internal rhythm of its own. They saw each other two or three nights during the week and always on the weekends. There was nothing formal or spoken about their arrangement; it just was. And then, as happens with so many similar relationships, it finally drifted into marriage, almost automatically, without either of them declaring their undying love for the other.

As you might have guessed, the marriage, for Ann anyway, was kind of anticlimactic. Now, instead of spending 60 percent of her nights with Barry, she was spending all of them. And still, most of her ego and sense of optimism were inextricably tied up in her career, which was booming. It wasn't too long before she was promoted to associate producer, a job that required occasional trips to California. Ann soon found herself in charge of her own music show, and this entailed working in close collaboration with several attractive young men. Ann's head began to whirl. Why had she ever gotten married? How constraining it was to travel to Los Angeles as a married woman, what with all the great-looking men one meets in the world of entertainment!

A situation developed between her and Lou, a curly-headed guitarist who wrote a great deal of the program's music. He invited Ann to spend the weekend with him at his beach house. She declined, frustrated and disappointed at having to do so. Yet several weeks later, a recording session was scheduled over an entire weekend, and Lou, of course, would be there for most of it. Ann grew more and more titillated. Who knew what would happen? She told Barry that he better find something to do for that Saturday and Sunday; perhaps, she suggested, he should even spend the weekend with his parents up in Connecticut. She was going to be so frantically busy that she didn't want to have to worry about whether he was being fed or not.

As the days rolled toward the appointed weekend, Ann became increasingly manic. Several times, while talking about her day at work (one of her favorite subjects), she mentioned Lou's name, what good music he wrote, how funny he was, what crazy hats he wore. Barry noted the slight hint of guilt in her eye every time she spoke about her new friend.

On the Friday morning before the recording session, Barry found himself unusually nervous. Ann was humming to herself in the shower. Barry cut himself while shaving. At work he could barely concentrate. Something was making him uncomfortable, and he wasn't quite sure he knew what it was. He called Ann to have lunch with him. She tried to decline, citing her crushing workload, but Barry persisted. "I won't be seeing you all weekend," he said.

They ate in a noisy delicatessen, Barry only toying with his food. "Is this Lou going to be working with you over the weekend?" he asked without looking up from his plate.

"Yeah. Why?"

"No reason."

As he walked Ann back to her office, Barry took her hand and held it tightly in his own, nor would he let go of it when they arrived at her building.

"Listen," he said. "I feel upset that I'm not going to see you this weekend. It's tearing me up inside."

"But why? You're going to be spending some time

with your parents. You said you've been looking forward to it."

"I don't want to spend time with my parents. I just want to be with you."

"I'm sorry, Barry. I set up these sessions over a month ago."

"You could cancel."

"But . . . but I really don't want to. I've been looking forward to it. We're going to lay down some great music. I wish you wouldn't be so upset."

"I can't help it." Barry paused, his face dark with fear, as if he were about to confess the most heinous of sins. "I . . . I . . . I'm worried something's going to happen, Ann, something that will hurt us very much." He looked at his feet in shame. "I don't want that. I love you, Ann. I love you very, very much."

"You love me?" Ann looked surprised, happy, awed. It was the first time in their nearly four years together that either of them had made such a declaration. He nodded his accord. "I don't want anything to happen to us, Ann. You mean too much to me."

Ann didn't cancel the sessions, but she did insist that Barry attend. She made every effort to make him feel loved and wanted and appreciated. This is not to say that she didn't feel a certain amount of regret that her flirtation with Lou didn't get more of a chance to flourish. But now armed with the knowledge, the *feeling,* of how deeply her husband loved her, she was better able to stand up to temptation, less willing to jeopardize her present relationship.

It took a crisis for Barry to confess the depth of his feeling for Ann. And when he did, instead of his avowal weakening his relationship with her, as he was so scared it might, it only strengthened it.

There is a message here. Your wandering mate, the husband or wife who seems to be drifting from you, may be searching for love. Have you verbalized the strength of your feelings to him or her? Today? Yesterday? The day before? And not only through touch or eye contact or vibrations, *but with words,* clearly and openly and articulately? As firmly as you may believe that your mate *knows* you love him or her, you may be wrong. To tell someone of your love convincingly and often (by which we mean several times a week, not a dozen times a day, which would become tiresome, oppressive, and ultimately empty) is one of the greatest compliments, one of the warmest strokes you can give another human being. Just think of the delicious feelings that wash over you when a child or parent or love-mate tells you that he or she loves you. Although they are merely words, there is nothing in the world quite like hearing them.

In the case of Barry and Ann, Barry erupted with his avowal of love because he could not help himself. He was in pain and was casting about for a way to assuage it. When he admitted to Ann his love for her, he believed that he was showing his weakness and thereby demeaning himself in her eyes. In actuality, pouring out his heart proved to be healing, and this surprised him.

Let us cite another case in which an open declaration of love brought two people together at a time when it seemed likely that they were about to break up.

Miranda dated Nathaniel on and off for about six months. The relationship was a happy and relaxed one, with both parties immensely enjoying one another's company. Nathaniel kept their meetings fairly platonic because he was engaged to a college senior in Minnesota, some several hundred miles from Chicago, the city in which both he and Miranda worked as lawyers. Perhaps Miranda would have preferred a deeper involvement than their occasional cuddling and light necking, but Nathaniel was so interesting and so entertaining that she did not press the issue for fear that she would drive him away. (And on one level she had to admit to herself that there were several pleasant if not slightly perverse aspects in assuming the role of "the other woman.")

Nevertheless, as one date with Nathaniel followed another, she began to find herself falling in love with him. He was wry, he was kind, and, unlike so many of the other men she dated, he wasn't always pawing at her. Perhaps it was this more than anything—the fact that instead of constantly hopping into bed like most young couples in their mid-twenties, they spent most of their time in conversation—that made her feel so close to him. Whatever the reason, as early June grew near, Miranda became increasingly forlorn. Nathaniel had informed her that he was taking the first two weeks of June to attend his fiancée's graduation and to help her move down to Chicago, where she would be sharing his apartment. He told Miranda that he thought it would be difficult for them to get together after that.

Their last date was spent at a cozy, local tavern at which they had had some of their best talks. Although Miranda laughed and chatted as usual, she was preoccupied with what she could do or say to make Nathaniel change his mind, to prevent him from driving up to Minnesota three days hence and in effect disappearing from her life forever.

She decided she would tell him she loved him, that he had become immensely important to her happiness. As a teenager she had resisted verbalizing her affection for fear she would be sneered at, taken advantage of. But over the past few years she had found that telling the men in her life about her positive feelings toward them had enhanced her relationships, often precipitating similar sentiments from the men. She would make comments like "I'm really having a good time with you," or "You look so handsome tonight," or "I feel proud walking into a restaurant on your arm." And these expressions almost always had a most positive effect.

Nathaniel walked her back to her apartment. They stood outside in the warm spring night, saying goodbye, the finality of it thick in the air. Suddenly, Miranda drew back. "You know, I'm not happy at all about this, Nathaniel," she said. "The idea of losing you, of not having you in my life forever and ever, fills me with incredible sadness. I've come to love being with you so much over the past months, I've grown so attracted to you, that the idea that I'll never have the chance to make love to you is unbearable." She shook her head mournfully.

"I didn't know you felt that way," he said, looking absolutely shocked.

"Well, I didn't at first. But I do now. If you don't come upstairs and spend the night with me, I will be the unhappiest woman on the face of the earth." She moved forward into his arms then and cried quietly on his shoulder. He went upstairs, spent the night in her bed, and stayed for keeps. They have now been married eight years.

Miranda had a strong hunch that Nathaniel would respond positively to her expression of love, and so she made the decision to tell him how she felt. Perhaps some would call this manipulative. But it is actually the *withholding* of a declaration of love that is manipulative. Withholding love is a form of game playing, for it is the suppression of a natural, healthy instinct in the misguided belief that it will make others beg for your affection. It is the giving and not the holding back of love that engenders love in those about you. And whether you are single, as Miranda was, or married, the principle is the same: To get love you must give it.

14   How to Deal with Your Mate's Affair

Many of you may very well have to deal with one of the more complex and painful problems that fate dishes out: your mate's affair. Infidelity is far from uncommon in a troubled marriage. Affairs may be surreptitious or aboveboard, as when one of the partners makes no attempt to disguise the fact that he or she is sleeping with and possibly in love with another. What can you do about it?

Our recommendation is that you explain that his or her infidelity is causing you great pain, that it is demeaning to you, that the affair is a violation of your marital vows. Then you tell, not ask, your mate to end it.

Naturally, the question comes up: But what if Ellen refuses? What if Larry responds, "Why? What are you going to do about it if I don't?"

Our suggestion is that you stick to your guns. Insist that the affair cease. The important thing is that your mate be made aware of your displeasure. He or she will not necessarily accede to your request, but, at the very least, there will be no doubt in your spouse' mind about how you regard his or her behavior.

Avoid discussing what you will or will not do if your mate continues to disregard your feelings, for unless you are willing to leave or to file for a legal separation, there is little sense in issuing an ultimatum. Remember, we don't want to threaten what we are not ready to carry out. It is better to choose the right theme and adhere to it with vehemence. Just as earlier we recommended that you demand that your mate stay with you, here we suggest that you tell your mate he or she must end his or her affair—nothing more, nothing less.

Stick with that premise as a dog hangs onto a bone. We realize how pained, how desperate, how jealous one can feel when one has to live, day in and day out, with a mate who is having an intimate relationship with another. The only comfort we can offer you is this: Our program often works, particularly if you are zealous and resolute in its execution.

As with many of the other suggestions in this book, we urge you to forge ahead, even if at times the process seems pointless. One never knows what effect one's actions are having behind the scenes, under the skin. We have found that a wandering mate (and sometimes even his or her lover) may suddenly lose interest in an affair at the very moment it seems most torrid.

So have your doubts, but proceed boldly forward despite them. Victory might be just around the corner. We would guess that a large percentage of all the couples you know have survived the trauma of an affair. Years later you may look back on this crisis as just another of life's little turbulences—like a bad case of bronchitis or water in the basement—and nothing more.

Withhold Sex

Early in the book we recommended that husbands and wives who are not communicating eschew intercourse until they've had a thorough conversation in which the problems between them have been aired. But what role should sex play in marriages that are much closer to a formal rupture, in which one mate is having an affair or has asked the other for a separation or even a divorce? Here we strongly urge you not to sleep with your mate until he or she convincingly announces his or her intention to give up any ideas of leaving.

To attempt to use sex to lure your mate back almost always winds up backfiring and leaves you feeling disappointed, used, and, most significantly, unsuccessful. Instead of reminding your estranged mate how wonderful you are, a round of lovemaking is much more likely to trigger his or her feelings of contempt and pity for you. *Esther is so desperate for me, she's still willing to submit, no matter how badly I treat her. How pathetic!* Or, *Doesn't Larry have any self-respect? He thinks I still love him just because I'm willing to sleep with him. Pitiful!*

We have also heard wounded husbands and wives tell us that they sleep with their departing mates only to relieve sexual frustration. *Why not?* he asks himself. *Wendy and I have always had good sex together. I won't deny that I'd love to have her back, but I know that just because she's willing to sleep with me doesn't mean that she loves me again. It's just good sex. I'm aware of that.*

Our experience would indicate that it's rarely good sex at all. Unfortunately (or perhaps fortunately), humans cannot dissociate their emotional feelings from sex the way animals can. During lovemaking, it is almost impossible for a man who is losing his wife to keep from thinking that maybe, just maybe, her ecstasy is more than a physical response.

At the same time, he is almost certainly aware that he is likely to have his hopes dashed. Thus, it is difficult for us to believe that he is really experiencing "good sex." Whether he is capable of admitting it to himself or not, he is probably using sex manipulatively, hoping against hope that it will lure his wife back, setting himself up for a crushing defeat by basking for a few stolen minutes of truly false intimacy between the sheets. And that is why we recommend that you do not attempt to use sex to win back a love. The aftertaste is both bitter and self-destructive.

The only exceptions to the above suggestion are those of you who can admit that the primary reason your mate is leaving you is that you almost always withhold sex. Then, perhaps, the most effective action you can take in winning him or her back is to initiate an evening full of glorious lovemaking. We know many spouses, husbands in particular, who would melt, would abandon in an instant any plans to leave, if only their mates would make love with them. One man has told us, "If my wife would sleep with me more than once a month, I would never even dream of leaving her. That's all I want."

We are aware, of course, that if it is extremely difficult for you to bear making love to your spouse, something between you is drastically wrong and urgently in need of repair. On the other hand, if it is simply a mixture of good old-fashioned fatigue, boredom, and anger that's been causing you to withhold sex, you must make an effort to find a spark of romance or lust or affection to bring you together again. A good evening of lovemaking with a love-starved mate can work wonders.

But back to our original point. Sex should not be used as a manipulative device designed to win back a love. Most of the time such a ploy has an effect opposite to the one desired.

Do Not Ask If There Is "Someone Else."

Assume there is. It is tragic and depressing to see how people kid themselves into believing that there isn't. Perhaps they use this kind of self-deception to help preserve their ego. The danger is that it may lure you into believing that the problem isn't as serious as it really is, that the actuality of your mate's leaving is not all that imminent.

Nonsense. There often is "someone else." Most people are reluctant to risk leaving the coziness of one relationship unless they can head right into another.

And even if there isn't a third party, believing that there is someone else will naturally make you more competitive, will bring out your best instincts for self-preservation.

However, you should never allow your mate to tell you about his or her lover. Your spouse will be tempted, partly out of the habit of sharing intimate details with you, and partly out of guilt. The problem is, if your spouse can get you to listen, he or she may feel you are giving the relationship your tacit blessing.

Don't be surprised then if your mate starts to tell you in glowing detail about a new lover or about what life has to offer "outside" your relationship together. Don't listen. Tell him or her you don't want to hear about it. Denounce the other man or woman in the most vitriolic terms, even if you haven't the faintest notion of who he or she is. After all, who would be so low as to try to steal someone else's mate? Your attitude will not only raise doubts in your spouse's mind about the moral fiber of whom he or she is getting involved with, but will indicate how strongly you are opposed to separation.

Your mate may counter that his or her new lover has professed undying adoration, loves him or her in a way that you never have. It's amazing how people can be taken in by mere words. You may want to cite the following statistics: Although 70 percent of those who divorce have an extramarital lover, only 15 percent actually marry that person.

No, your mate's paramour doesn't love him or her as you do, for he or she hasn't taken the giant step of marrying your spouse. Will he? Will she? The odds are overwhelmingly against it. You, on the other hand, have married your mate, demonstrating a willingness to accept and to compromise that your spouse is probably wildly underestimating. Your relationship may not be perfect, but having been time-tested, it is a known quantity. The other relationship is not, and there is no reason to believe that those who are so desperate as to try to usurp another's husband or wife can be counted on to make good on their words.

A middle-aged man we interviewed described—with delight, we might add—how he won his wife away from another suitor by continually referring to his rival as a fool.

Judd and Nicole had been dating for several weeks when Nicole was invited by an old college roommate to spend the week in Boston. While there, she went out on a blind date with a student at Harvard Law School. He was a brilliant, dashing man who wore natty clothes and had a way with words. Nicole was smitten, and after spending forty-eight dazzling, romantic hours with him responded with manic enthusiasm when, in a moment of sudden passion, he asked her to marry him. Several days after she returned home to Washington, D.C., Judd called to ask her to join him for dinner. Nicole accepted but only to explain that she could no longer go out with him because she was now engaged to a wonderful new man in Boston.

"Wonderful, my ass!" answered Judd. "He sounds like a fool to me, asking someone to marry him after two lousy days. He must be desperate, a real loser. Probably no one else will have him." He then launched into a witty but nonetheless savage attack upon this man whom he'd never met in his entire life. "Probably has dandruff and bad breath."

"No, no, no," protested Nicole.

But Judd would not let her finish. "I can see him now, all greedy-faced and narcissistic, boring you with tales of wonderful law briefs and the joys of being a lawyer's bride. God!" And no matter how hard Nicole tried to defend her new fiancé, Judd would cut her off.

"I must save you from this numbskull," he said, "or at least show you a good time during your last few months of freedom. I would feel like a heel if I didn't at least give it a try."

"Oh, alright," said Nicole. "We'll continue to go out but no more sleeping together."

Over the next few weeks, Judd pressed his attack, ridiculing his unknown and unknowing competitor every time Nicole tried to bring up his name. "I don't want to hear about the moron," he'd say, clapping his hands over his ears. After a while, Nicole began to giggle at the little game, particularly after returning from a trip to Boston.

"How was the little dandy?" Judd would ask. And before Nicole had a chance to answer, he'd supply his own. "Impotent as usual, I bet. And boring, God, how boring those lawyers are!"

Before long, Nicole would be near hysterics, laughing until tears came to her eyes over Judd's rambling, ranting attack upon her intended. Within six weeks, the strategy had taken its effect. Nicole resumed sleeping with Judd. Within three months, she broke off her engagement to the law student. Today, seventeen years later, Judd still pokes fun at the man he has never met; and Judd's wife, Nicole, responds with glee over the utter absurdity of it all.

Why, we asked Judd, did he ever resort to such an unusual maneuver?

"I'm not sure" was his answer. "I was angry. I wanted to hit back, even though I didn't know this fellow from Adam. I also felt panicked. I didn't want to lose Nicole. This supposed marriage was only a few months away. My feeling was that if I just sat around and behaved myself, I would lose her. I sensed that I had to take action—fast—and to denounce the man was the only assertive thing I could think of. Plus, I knew that if I kept on, sooner or later I would hit upon his flaws, and that when I did, Nicole's facial expression would give it away, which it did. Then I exploited the hell out of it. Finally, it was a lot of fun. It helped me get my hurt and frustration out."

Do you think you could do the same? It might be worth a try. And, as Judd said, at the very least it's a lot of fun.

Be Relentless and Ruthless

You owe your competition nothing. A feeble sense of "rightness" on your part, an artificial adherence to fair play, will undermine your quest. Win now, apologize for any unseemly behavior later.

Naturally, we do not want you to do anything that violates your bedrock sense of morality. But, at the same time, we would like you to test yourself, to see if you are capable of exploring ways of acting and talking that may be a part of your latent or heretofore *unflexed* repertory of responses.

Until now you've never been in a battle quite like this one. But make no mistake: If you are fighting to keep a wandering lover, you are in a battle; and it is quite appropriate to resort to actions that under less trying times would be alien to you. So be it. You are at war. Proceed accordingly, which may mean having to stop acting like the nice, upstanding boy or girl your parents raised you to be. To keep your mate, you may, temporarily anyway, have to metamorphose into a tiger.

Recount to your spouse all the reasons he or she would be a fool to leave you: You *love* your husband; your competitor may only like him. You will be faithful to your wife; her new lover may cheat on her and finally desert her. Your time and affection will be limited if a final break occurs. Point out the financial pitfalls of a separation. Be well versed in them, and exaggerate if you must. The fear of the financial strain of divorce is a powerful deterrent.

Leave no stone unturned. Dig down and ferret out all your mate's secret fears. Bankruptcy? Baldness? Impotence? Loss of attractiveness? Now ask yourself: Is there any way to exploit these fears? For example, you love your wife even though each year she sprouts a new varicose vein. Will her new lover be as accepting? And what about your husband's long-standing inability to keep an erection? Will his girlfriend be as understanding, as patient as you? Probably not. And if she abandons him, what makes him think you will still be around to take him back?

Perhaps it has occurred to you to contact your mate's lover either by phone or mail. We have mixed feelings about this course of action and therefore cannot offer any definitive advice. The risks are obvious: You may be ignored; you may further alienate your spouse; and, depending upon the person with whom you are dealing, you may even be exposing yourself to physical violence. On the other hand, we have seen instances in which one spouse was openly cheating, while unconsciously hoping the other would intervene. It is almost as if the wandering spouse were saying, "If you really care about me, let me see you do something."

If you *do* make a personal decision to contact your mate's paramour, it is essential to use extreme discretion. You might say or write something like this: *Please recognize that my wife means everything to me, and I don't want to lose her. I have insisted that she stop seeing you and now ask that you stop seeing her. I am sure that if you had any idea of the unhappiness you are causing our family, you would realize that this affair simply isn't worth it.*

Whatever you do, under no circumstances should you attempt to frighten or intimidate your spouse's lover, nor should you telephone repeatedly or at inconvenient or embarrassing times nor send a barrage of letters—this would be harassment, which is against the law. There is no law, however, against conveying a sincere and honest request.

Does all this sound like dirty business? Perhaps you saw the film *Mon Oncle d'Amérique*. In it is recounted the life of a French assistant minister of culture. He falls in love with a young, beautiful woman, and leaves his wife and children for her. Distraught, the wife visits the mistress one day while the husband is out.

"You must let us have him back," says the wife. "I am dying of cancer. It will be only for a few months." Without explaining why, the guilt-ridden mistress asks the cabinet minister to leave. Crushed, he returns to his wife.

Five years pass. The young woman accidentally meets the cabinet minister in the countryside. He looks wonderful. "And what happened to your poor wife?" asks his former mistress.

"Oh, she is fine," he replies.

"Not dead yet!"

"Oh, no. Not in the least. She is thriving."

And thus the mistress discovers she has been hoodwinked. Enraged, she makes a play for her old lover, but it is too late. The planets and stars have shifted, the moon is on the horizon, and the cabinet minister is in love with his wife again.

We momentarily rest our case.

15   Insist on One Year

Up to this juncture in the book, we've concentrated mainly on the early signs and symptoms of marital trouble. Now we'll consider what to do when your mate has announced his or her intention to move out.

It is really amazing how we human beings lose perspective in the heat of passion. Even in the best of marriages, we argue with our husband or wife, and we think it is all over between us. Never mind that we have argued like this before and have come out of it just fine. At the height of emotion, the anger seems implacable, the bitterness unending, the rejection permanent. The person sitting across the table was the center of your world just hours before. Now you're convinced it's all over between you. Strange? No, just human nature.

No one seriously contemplates separating after a couple of fights. The *thought* may well flash through our minds, but it is quickly whisked away. It usually takes years of disagreement to bring matters to the breaking point.

A person announces that he's leaving and assures himself that he has made a reasoned decision. Yet it's tough to exercise good judgment when one sees the world through tears of rage or bitterness. The decision to leave, no matter how carefully thought out, is rarely made with a dispassionate heart.

But the problem is not just one of emotion. It is also one of perspective. Things between you and your wife look impossible today. That's today. They'll look a lot different next month. Not necessarily better, but surely different. What seems like an insurmountable obstacle now will be forgotten later. A new problem will appear in its place. People are not static, and neither are relationships.

Now, please don't take anything we've said up until now to mean that "everything will be all right." Without a lot of work, it won't be. We've simply said that if you can hold on, there's likely to be a whole new ball game. Once your mate is out the door, though, it will be a lot harder to do the work that has to be done.

The point is that you need time. Time to maneuver. Time for both of you to gain a new perspective. Time for emotions to cool and issues to be reflected upon. Time for you to change. Of course, time alone is not enough. If you can gain time, though, you've gained a giant advantage.

Now here's our major piece of advice: If your mate informs you that he or she wants a separation, ask for time. If necessary, demand it!

You've been having troubles for over a year. He insists that it's over. He tells you that he's leaving. Make him an offer that he can't refuse.

"No!" you shout. "I won't let this happen so easily. You mean too much to me. For those sixteen years we've been married, I demand one year to straighten it out. If I fail, I'll let you go in peace."

Tell him there's a lot at stake. Recount all that you've invested in each other over the years. Your friends and relatives. Your home. Everything you've accumulated together.

Don't absolve him of his responsibilities in a misguided attempt to appear noble. You are not laying a guilt trip on someone by reminding him of the damage that can result from his impulsive actions. "I'm asking for almost nothing. Just a year. You owe it to the kids to give it this one last chance." Tell him you've got a plan to make it work. Reassure him that you'll take the blame if it fails and that you won't try to hold him if he gives you a year.

Now, what have you really given up? Nothing. He doesn't need your permission to leave. He's about to go anyway. He may not like your deal because he may not want to be stopped. Maybe there's another woman waiting for him. Maybe he just wants to get it over with. But, like it or not, he probably won't be able to turn you down. It's a hard deal for a reasonable man to refuse.

So I can get him to stay for a year, you think. *What good will that do?* Let us relate a brief parable.

Many years ago, in a far-off land, lived a king and a sorcerer. The sorcerer had fallen out of favor in the court. He was arrested and sentenced to death. All pleas for his pardon were unavailing.

On the day of his planned execution, the sorcerer asked the king for an audience, and it was granted. "My King," said he, "I shall not plead for mercy. However, I shall show you how it will be to your advantage to spare my life."

"Hah!" replied the king. "Up to your old tricks again. I'm tired of them. How can it be to my advantage to let you live?"

"If you will give me but one year," replied the sorcerer, "confined in your castle, I shall make your horse talk. And you will then be the most famous monarch in the world. If I do not do as I say, you may kill me after twelve months, and I shall not object."

"Hmm," mused the king. "My horse talk. Yes, indeed, I would be the most famous king ever if my horse could talk. All right, Sorcerer. You have one year. Not one day more. If you do as you promise, you are free. If you fail, I swear by my crown you shall die."

The sorcerer's close friend, a duke, heard of this

strange arrangement and sneaked up to the dungeon late that night.

"Oh, my friend," said he. "You are indeed a fool. I know, and you know, that you do not have the power to make animals speak. Now you will surely die."

The sorcerer put his hand on the duke's shoulder. "Dear Duke," he said. "I have a year. Many things can happen in a year. The king might die. Or I might die. And who knows? In a year, perhaps the horse might talk."

Even if you ask for it, some of you won't get a year. Insist on six months. If you can't get six, demand three. The overriding principle is to buy time, as much of it as possible. If worst comes to worst and your mate moves out, then insist on meeting regularly for lunch or dinner so you can continue to talk about the two of you. Even the most embittered spouse won't fail to be impressed by your persistence. Even the most angry will realize that it is in his or her self-interest to maintain a dialogue with you about the finances or the children.

Insist, Don't Beg, That Your Mate Stay

It has been our observation that much too high a percentage of those husbands and wives who are being left and who are desperately unhappy about it simply roll over and give up. They do not fight back. "Things are not working out," they hear themselves being told. "We ought to separate, for a while anyway. It will be better for both of us."

And instead of replying, "Not on your life, we're in this thing together for keeps," they break into tears, want to know what they've done wrong, and ask meekly if there's anybody else. Then, at their estranged mate's direction, they proceed to hire a lawyer to facilitate the separation. Some are even manipulated into convincing themselves that it is they, and not the leaving spouse, who want the marriage to end. How self-destructive! How at odds with what many must really want to say and do!

Our prescription is to tell your mate, firmly and without hysterics, that you do not want him or her to leave. You are not strangers. There is no need to stand on ceremony, to keep a stiff upper lip as your spouse packs his or her bags.

Perhaps both of you have forgotten that sometime in the past you pledged to honor and obey one another, in sickness and in health, for better or for worse, till death do you part. Chances are you meant those words when you said them three or five or a dozen years ago. What about now?

Has your mate come to view the sanctity of your marital contract too cavalierly? It is so easy in these fast-moving times of instant intimacy and pop solutions to difficult problems for a wandering spouse to come to the conclusion that a long-term marriage is obsolete and to assume that you feel the same way, too.

If this is the case in your marriage, now is the time to communicate to your mate just how important the relationship is to you. The more seriously you take it, the more seriously he will have to take it. Realize that you may never have another chance. Once two people physically separate, it becomes that much more difficult for them to get back together. It is one thing not to be getting along well; it is another thing entirely to be living on opposite sides of town.

Do not be lured into a so-called trial separation. These arrangements occasionally work out well; but more often than not, trial separations backfire, and here's why: The trial separation provides an illusion of freedom. Moving out does offer instant relief from a highly pressured situation, but the freedom is only a mirage. The leaving spouse thinks that he or she is comparing married life with single life, and the latter seems quite appealing. He or she is, in fact, comparing the worst of the marriage with the best of the unattached state. The marriage seems horrible; the new vistas, unlimited.

No wonder many couples who physically separate choose not to reconcile: They're living in a temporary but unreal world. A year down the pike, though, divorce may not seem so sweet. The leaver may see the dark side of freedom, namely, loneliness. But by then it is often too late.

Stay in close contact with your spouse no matter how painful it might be. Don't agree to trial separations, even brief ones. Don't avoid your spouse, and don't let your spouse avoid you.

If nothing you've tried up to this point has dismantled your mate's mounting momentum to leave, you must now take the boldest, most uncompromising stand of your life: "I insist that you stay." As one caller told us on a talk show, "When you are fighting for your marriage, you are fighting for your life."

Now is not the time to mince words, nor is it the time to maintain a facade of ladylike or gentlemanly good manners. You are being dealt a brutal blow. Respond with equal force, not with violence but with vehemence. If you must, plant yourself in front of the door and declare, "No, I won't have it. I want your love, and whether you know it or not, you want mine. I won't let you hurt us like this. I won't let you destroy us." Your mate must understand that you believe he is being as destructive to himself as to you. Do not hide behind a facade of kindness. Do not try to comprehend your spouse's side of the story. If you nod your understanding while your wife is informing you that she's fallen in love with someone else or while your husband is explaining how he's outgrown the relationship, then you are actually absolving him or her of any wrongdoing. You are making it easier for your spouse to go.

Nor should you burst into tears or berate your spouse with a long list of his or her faults and failures. Do the one thing that he or she wasn't counting on. State your intention of refusing to let him or her go.

A young woman we interviewed described the circumstances under which she broke off with her husband of three years. Their anniversary was imminent, and she was feeling increasingly numb at the prospect of the years going by as she remained trapped in an unfulfilling marriage. The original spark of romance she had felt for her husband had dimmed considerably. Nevertheless, she felt conscience-bound to continue. Her husband seemed so dependent upon her, so adoring. She put on the best face she could yet was not able to conceal her misgivings. Over their anniversary dinner her husband inquired why she seemed so depressed. "Have I done anything wrong?" he asked.

It is easy enough from our vantage point, of course, to see that he was leading with his chin. And as you might have predicted, the young man's query triggered an outpouring of doubt from his reluctant wife. She wasn't sure they should stay together, she said. She wasn't feeling enough in love, she was feeling too hemmed in. The young man started to sniffle. "Oh, God, you don't want to stay married to me. You don't love me. I knew it," he wailed. "I just knew it."

"Maybe it would be better if I left," said the woman. Packing a small suitcase, she departed within a half-hour and moved in with several women friends on the other side of town.

She expressed amazement to us at how easy her husband had made it for her to break things off. "If he had gotten angry and said to me, 'Don't think you can leave me like this,' I'm pretty sure I never would have split. I had doubts about the marriage, yes, but I'm the kind of person who always has gotten scared and depressed and unsure of myself before undertaking any big change in my life, like switching jobs or picking a college. Whenever anyone around me has been forceful or shown leadership, I've been only too happy to go along. If Les had shown more determination, he could easily have swayed me. I needed him to be firm. In fact, when I think back on it, I realize how incredibly easy it would have been for him to have kept me right there in my chair. Just the right few words would have done it."

The point to grasp here is that you have every right to put up a fuss, not to go meekly, but to oppose your mate's intention to abandon you. And not only do you have the right, but you may very well find that simply insisting that he or she stay is the single most effective step you can take in winning back a love. When the chips are down, you must tell your mate you do not, under any circumstances, want him or her to go. It is awesome how quickly this kind of firmness on your part can dissipate any hazy, romantic musings of what it will be like to be single again. We human beings are as much creatures of infatuation as we are of good sense.

And don't worry how silly it might seem if he or she temporarily walks out in the process. Stick to your party line: "I insist that you stay."

Life is perverse. Just when the oldest, simplest, most direct appeals seem most futile, they begin to work. You hear the same commercial two dozen times. The twenty-fifth time, for some reason you cannot fathom, you suddenly find yourself being persuaded by the advertisement's message.

It Is Easier for Your Mate to Stay Than Leave

No matter how determined your mate seems to leave, it is almost always easier for him or her to stay than to go. Biologically, your mate's inertia, familiarity with present surroundings, and fear of the unknown are on your side. The human animal, as all animals, is more attracted to safety than freedom, for freedom is always accompanied by danger.

Use this principle to your advantage. State your case constantly, vigorously, thoroughly. Mention to your mate the wonderful aspects of your life together: the happy times with the children, the cozy, cuddly sex, your warm accepting manner, the delicious meals, the orderliness of your home. Do everything in your power to tip the scale in your favor. Overwhelm your competition. Drown it out.

Recount for your mate the pitfalls and difficulties of leaving. Her new lover may grow dissatisfied and leave in turn. He may miss you and your support much more than he ever anticipated, could get mugged at a new address, receive a heating bill that is triple the present one, become physically ill over guilt at having deserted you, fall in with a bad crowd, catch herpes, etc., etc. Even if you feel silly, persevere. The object is to make it more attractive for your mate to stay than to leave.

Also recognize that your mate may unconsciously be longing to be called back. Or consciously, too, like a child who is threatening to leave home and wants nothing more than to be asked to come back. A one-night stand with the golf pro or secretary may have gotten out of hand. Without being able to admit it, your mate may be longing for you to put your foot down and demand that he or she stop this nonsense so that the two of you can get on with the business of life together.

You might want to put it this way to your spouse: If he or she leaves to establish a new life that winds up being only 10 or 15 percent better than the one you presently share, he or she is striking a bad bargain, for to give up the good things you have together for such a questionable improvement surely cannot be worth the trauma and expense of leaving.

And while you're at it, remember that the winning back of a love may not be the all-or-nothing, black-and-white, open-and-shut case you expect it to be. The process may unfold over a period of weeks, seasons, years, decades. It may wind up being part of a maintenance program, as insulin is to a diabetic. On one level, one could argue that we are all continually losing and winning back the same person, many times, even in the course of a day. So be persistent, always persistent. Keep the pressure on, more than your competition can or would even think to do. You have greater need and love on your side. That can be an enormous boost to winning.

16   Specificity

Let us assume that you have asked your husband to give you twelve months to change, and he has agreed. Now what do you do? If you don't want your mate to wake up one morning two or three months down the line, thinking to himself, *This feels just like our relationship* before *the trial period*, then you must get him to tell you what he wants—not in vague generalizations but with tangible specifics. If he waffles, pin him down.

Does your husband want more time for golf? Does your wife think you should spend more time with the kids? Does she feel overburdened? Work out a program, with her agreement, on how the two of you can get more fun, more play, into her life. Ask her what chores you can take over. The gardening? No, she likes that. But she could use more help with the baby. Fine, you'll agree to babysit for your one-year-old every Wednesday night and Saturday afternoon so that she can take ballet class. Would she like that? Yes, very much. There, that wasn't so bad, was it?

And your husband? Why does he want to leave? Because you never initiate intercourse, he says, not once in the last two years. It makes him feel so unloved. He wants to find a woman who appreciates him more. Well, what about it? To save your marriage, can you bring yourself to snuggle up to your husband once or twice a month? Maybe that is all that is needed.

Sounds absurd, doesn't it, that a solution could be so simple, that the mere sliding across one and a half feet of bedding several times a year could heal a wounded marriage? And yet, in more cases than you'd expect, it is just such a simple, specific, tangible action on one spouse's part that is needed to bring the other partner back into the relationship.

Some of you might be thinking that it is not the act so much as the gesture, the willingness to compromise, that can dissipate a hostile partner's anger. We think it is both. The important point is that you are willing to change. Many people aren't. Many find it too humiliating or too difficult to alter their behavior. And those are the people who tend to do poorly in human relationships. But those who can adapt, those who can fathom what they are doing wrong and have the intelligence and strength to correct it, are the people whose marriages tend to last. It is downright Darwinian. Those species that can adapt survive. Those that can't, don't.

Let us examine the case of Bill and Madeline. Bill is a highly sexed individual who enjoys making love every night. The act holds great significance for him, for he sees it as the ultimate expression of love. To Madeline, sex has neither the same deep meaning nor appeal. She is satisfied to have intercourse once a week and sees it more as sport, closer to dancing or card playing than a manifestation of the intensity of her love. She has always felt most affectionate when holding hands with Bill or reading together in front of the fire. And there, in a nutshell, is one of the classic divides that exists in many marriages. It is how that chasm is bridged that frequently determines whether a couple stays together or not, whether husband and wife live in harmony or not.

In Bill and Madeline's case, their different attitudes toward sex almost tore them apart. During the early years, Madeline was usually willing to make love whenever Bill wanted. Sometimes, after sleeping late on Saturday or Sunday morning, she would wake him up by nibbling on his ear, caressing his back. She was younger, stronger then, felt more attractive, and had not yet borne the two boys who soon came to take up most of her time and energy.

But as the years went by, Madeline's forays onto Bill's side of the bed grew increasingly infrequent until they disappeared altogether. Madeline didn't even realize it. She knew she loved Bill deeply and was sure that he was aware of it.

He wasn't. His wife's occasional advances had been blissful to him, an indication of her passionate love. Their disappearance left a terrible void. Night after night Bill would wait for her touch, but it never came. The couple had intercourse only when he initiated it, and even then Madeline often resisted his advances because she was too tired or not in the mood. Bill grew angrier and angrier, and felt increasingly unloved. *I will find a girlfriend,* he decided, *someone who finds me sexy, someone whom I really turn on.*

And he did—a young receptionist in the garment business where he worked as a salesperson. The affair was heavenly, and it seemed to Bill that when they were alone, Linda could hardly keep her hands off him. He made up his mind to move in with her, and one Friday morning, as he was getting ready for work, informed his wife of his decision.

Madeline was dumbfounded. How could this be? Yes, there had been some friction about their differences over the importance of sex in their marriage. But she knew they basically loved one another, and she was not about to lose this man with whom she had created two wonderful children and a home full of warmth and stability.

"You cannot leave me," she insisted. "You must at least give me the consideration of seeing the priest together." Bill could tell that his wife was adamant, and without quite realizing it consciously, he was pleased that the marriage seemed so important to her. It made him feel loved, and he agreed to try to talk things out with Father K.

Bill explained how his wife almost never made sexual overtures to him. Madeline agreed that this was true but said she never realized how important they were to Bill. "Well, they are," he said, "not every night but at least once in a while."

"How often?" asked the priest, an elderly man who had heard this complaint many times before.

"Oh, maybe once a month," said Bill.

"Can you manage that?" Father K. asked Madeline.

"Sure," she replied. "I'd enjoy it."

"Okay, then, you're to initiate intercourse with your husband at least once a month," he ordered Madeline. And to Bill, "I want you to stop your affair. Agreed?"

"Agreed."

The plan worked. Madeline kept her end of the bargain by initiating intercourse occasionally, and apparently that was all Bill needed. His affair ended immediately. His wife's advances were far more satisfying to him than the attentions of the young receptionist. Madeline, of course, has to remind herself every so often to make sure she is being affectionate enough. It is not a role that comes naturally to her. But the compromise is well worth the effort, for a sound monogamous marriage is essential to her happiness.

What's the moral here? Now that you have got your mate to stick around for a while by promising to change, get her to tell you exactly what she wants. Press her to be specific—less "You're not considerate enough" and more "I want you to be home on time for dinner and shave more often and take me out once a week." In other words, insist that your spouse give you one or several real, tangible, doable tasks. And then accomplish them.

I have no intention of changing my personality for anyone, not even my spouse, you might be thinking, and, *I couldn't change my basic character even if I wanted to.* But personality change is not the issue. Even if it were possible, it is neither necessary nor particularly desirable. We are talking here about changing your behavior, not selling out or caving in or giving up. You can change the way you act without relinquishing your selfhood.

It is essential that you know what your spouse wants, in absolutely specific terms, for that is the only way you can begin to act differently. Do you remember the following old ditty?

> Women's faults are many,
> Men have only two:
> Everything they say
> And everything they do.

You can't be expected to change everything you say and everything you do, but it is possible to alter the specific ways in which you behave.

Say you are a demonstrative, outgoing woman, an amateur actress, and the center of attention at every social occasion. Your corporate executive husband is disgusted with your public displays of emotion, especially when you have had a little too much to drink. You cannot, and should not, attempt to transform yourself into a nun. On the other hand, you are probably capable of more decorum and less drinking, particularly when you are with your husband and his associates. There is ample opportunity for you to express yourself on stage, so you should restrain yourself at official company dinners. Don't be surprised if a 10 percent change in your behavior is all that he wants. Now in his eyes you're "lively," not "wacko."

Imagine you are a man who worries a great deal. Try as your wife might, she has not been able to convince you that disaster doesn't lurk around every corner. She is fed up with your fretting, and has begun to see your constant expressions of gloom and doom as a cornerstone in your future life together. You yourself recognize that your anxieties are unfounded, but you can't get them out of your mind.

Your mind is your own private place. We all have a basic right to worry privately, but that doesn't mean that we have a right to burden everyone else with all our fears. No one can expect you not to worry, but you can learn to limit your hand wringing and keep some of your worries to yourself.

A final point about specificity. Your spouse may couch his demands in specific terms but produce such a laundry list of complaints that he might as well fault "everything you say and everything you do." Don't be intimidated by a laundry list; if your spouse provides one, he is willing to negotiate. Your job now is to distinguish what he really wants from those little extras he has thrown in to bolster his case.

Examine the list. We can assure you that your mate does not expect you to comply with all his demands. It is your task, therefore, to isolate the real problems. Let's say she says, "You leave your gum wrappers on the floor and you don't put the cap on the toothpaste and you don't replace the toilet paper and you're always at your mother's house . . ." and on and on. You know that she has never liked your mother, whom she regards as intrusive and overbearing. Use your instinct. Venture a guess: The problem is your mother, not the gum wrappers or the toothpaste or the toilet paper. You don't have to stop loving your mother. But perhaps you should spend less time with her and more time with your wife. If you do so, you might find that the rest of the laundry list disappears like a cloud of soap bubbles.

Separate what can be changed from what cannot. You can dress more attractively; you cannot become a beauty queen. You can be a better carpenter; you cannot become a millionaire. You can act more friendly at social gatherings; you cannot become the life of the party. It is quite unlikely that your spouse really wants a total overhaul, no matter how vehemently he expresses himself. A marginal change is usually quite sufficient to turn your marriage around. The sad thing is that people become inflexible in times of marital stress. They stubbornly cling to their sense of "personhood," and refuse to give that inch that would make all the difference in the world.

Opposites Don't Necessarily Stay Attracted

Don't be surprised if, when you ask your mate to be specific, he or she turns on you for the very things that seemed to have attracted him or her in the first place. Those same traits your spouse found most endearing when you were courting may now have become the worst sticking points.

Dexter came from a respected and very proper WASP family. His father was a judge, and his mother was chairperson of the DAR. An only child, Dexter went to an exclusive prep school, then Princeton University and Harvard Law School. His friends joked that he had been born in a three-piece suit. He might as well have been. Dexter was the very picture of a perfect gentleman by the age of twelve.

Fran could not have come from a background more different. Her parents were immigrant Italians who were fun-loving and boisterous, and both were professional singers. Fran had nine attractive, loud, and effervescent brothers and sisters. They were loud because you had to scream to make yourself heard in their household. Dinner time was a nonstop marathon of yelling, laughing, singing, wine, and good food.

Dexter met Fran at an auto-repair shop. He was waiting for his diesel engine to be tuned and was attracted by the red-haired woman in the red convertible. They sat together for a few hours and were immediately taken with each other. Dexter had never met a woman so vital, so exuberant, so filled with energy. Fran was enchanted by Dexter's quiet good looks, his brains, and his sense of stability. They married six months later.

Five years down the road, Fran and Dexter were having trouble and were not so sure they were still in love. They no longer talked much to each other but spent a lot of time complaining to friends. It is instructive to hear their complaints.

First, Dexter: "Fran is a nut," he griped. "She's a wild woman, so uninhibited that she's a constant embarrassment."

Now Fran: "You just can't get a rise out of Dex. What a stiff! I've never met such a cold fish."

The significant point is that both partners are describing the very behaviors that attracted them to each other but cast in a totally different light. When they were in love, Fran was "vivacious"; now, she is a "wild woman." While things were good, Dexter was "stable" and "reliable"; now, he is a "cold fish."

What often initially attracts us to a member of the opposite sex are those qualities we lack in ourselves. During times of marital crisis, however, those same qualities may become the most irksome, particularly if they are the polar opposites of our own.

Perhaps you are trying to rekindle your partner's interest by falling back on old charms, by emphasizing those very things that once turned your partner on. Keep up the energy but try changing direction: Downplay the differences and become a little more like him or her. Dexter, for example, might take a shot at being more adventurous and relax his officious style. Fran could do well with a showing of sobriety and some earthy common sense.

No one expects a radical personality change. Once again, a small shift in behavior is often enough to bring you and your mate back into harmony, to get you functioning together again in a healthy and mutually satisfying way.

17   Steadfastness

There is a lot to be learned from the old story of the tortoise and the hare: Slow but steady wins the race. Let's rephrase this famous fable: If you can't outsprint the competition, then get yourself ready for a lot of long-distance running.

Let's say your husband seems a bit too interested in his pretty new secretary, a woman young enough to be your daughter . . . or his. Just the medicine, he thinks, for his impending mid-life crisis. Or your wife can't seem to stay away from this musclebound tennis instructor at the Y, a man who seems to make her forget her cellulite. How can you compete with that?

Perhaps with less difficulty than you might think. Most partners who fear being left underestimate the enormous tactical advantage their position as spouse provides. Like any tactical advantage, though, you've got to know how to use it, and you must be patient. Otherwise, you'll have no advantage at all.

Consider for a moment why people get married, and why, for the most part, they stay married. Looks, shared interests, sex, money, and so on. But more basic than these, we maintain, is the universal human need for security, for having one person to depend on through bad times and good.

As small children, our sense of well-being is largely

determined by the kind of love our parents give us. Ideally, this love should be constant and unselfish. A small child is weak and helpless, and he knows it. He is painfully aware of how dependent he is. He needs to be able to count on his parents . . . unconditionally.

If parents are unreliable, children grow up to be anxious and insecure adults. When mother and father can be counted on, youngsters have a much better chance of developing at least a modicum of self-confidence. Yet even under the best of circumstances, we never outgrow our need to depend on others. We marry in the hope that we have found that one human being who will be steadfast in his or her commitment to care for our needs.

The need for caring and for steadfastness does not change throughout life. That need may not be obvious to the man or woman who is in the heat of a passionate affair. Infatuation tends to make us feel grandiose, invulnerable, above petty human concerns. But the heady mist of infatuation soon clears, and we are again face to face with our sense of insecurity and weakness, our basic human vulnerability.

When Tevyah, in *Fiddler on the Roof*, asks his wife if she loves him, she replies, "For twenty-five years I've cleaned your house, raised your kids . . ." and then goes on to catalogue every way in which she has been an intimate part of his life. "If that's not love," she observes, "what is?"

This is where you, the spouse, have the hands-down advantage, because you are there, because you have been part of his or her life. Now you've got to exploit this advantage. You've got to *demonstrate* your caring and your steadfastness. If you succeed, your spouse will get the point that you, and only you, really care. You and only you are his or her true friend.

Diane and Larry were childhood sweethearts who dated throughout college. Larry graduated first and took a job as an executive in a construction company. He was wildly in love with Diane and couldn't wait until she graduated so that they could marry. During her senior year he gave her a beautiful engagement ring. Then she began to panic.

Diane felt that she wasn't ready for marriage. She felt unsure of herself. She avoided Larry's phone calls and often broke dates. Finally, she returned the ring and insisted on seeing other men. Larry put up with this for a few months, then declared that he had had enough. He officially broke the engagement and told Diane that they were through.

As the months passed, Diane felt depressed and dissatisfied with the men she dated. Sure, some of them were attractive enough, and many were quite appealing. But none of them were Larry. They were just dates. Larry was her best friend and had been so for many years. She realized that she was in love with him and that she missed him terribly.

She tried to call to tell him how wrong she had been, but his phone had been changed to an unlisted number. She left messages for him at work, but these went unanswered. She wrote a long letter declaring her love. The letter was returned with a two-word reply: "We're through."

Diane realized that complex reasoning would no longer work. Larry was skeptical of everything she said and cynically twisted all her best arguments. It was clear that Larry was angry and hurt. He had lost confidence in her. He no longer trusted her.

Diane had an inspiration. Cleverness wasn't working, so why not try something simple? She ran to the stationery store and bought one hundred friendship cards. She then penned an identical message on each:

I am sorry.
I was wrong.
I want you back.
I love you.

She carefully addressed and stamped all one hundred, then piled them in a neat stack on her desk. She removed the top card from the pile and dropped it into the mailbox. The next day, she mailed the second card. And the next day, the third. No extra messages. No telephone calls. No letters.

There was no response, but Diane persevered. At least the cards weren't being returned. Thirty in a month. Sixty in two months. She began to despair as the third month drew to a close. Eighty-nine cards down. Eleven to go.

Then, on the ninetieth day, when Diane absentmindedly went to mail a card, she opened her door and Larry was standing there.

"Okay. You win. Let's get married."

What made this silly trick work when everything else had failed? Larry had been disillusioned. He had invested a great deal in the relationship and had assumed that Diane was his. When she backed away, he did not understand. He saw her as insincere, as fickle. He became bitter and angry. He mistrusted her and received her attempts at reconciliation with skepticism. *Sure she talks a good game*, he thought. *Just more indecision.*

Then the cards started coming, like clockwork. At first, Larry thought they were ridiculous. He read the same simple message day after day and couldn't imagine what had come into the mind of this woman who had always been so sophisticated. A card arrived each day for a week. Then two on Monday and one more on each succeeding day. Week after week.

She must be some kind of nut to keep this up, Larry thought, with a mixture of amusement and perplexity. He saved the cards and compared them. All identical. He rushed home each day to be sure there was another. There always was. He didn't understand it, but his anger faded and his old feelings for Diane reemerged. *That woman won't give up*, he thought, and laughed despite himself. And finally he gave in.

The cards were just a gimmick, of course. Their explicit message was a simple and rather meaningless statement. Day after day after day. But the point was finally hammered home: *I want you back and I won't*

*give up. I'll prove to you that I mean what I say and I'll
stick to my guns. And I won't change my mind. You can
count on me.*

Quite by coincidence, we heard of another demonstration of constancy, quite similar but under very
different circumstances.

A man we knew was hospitalized for a serious
illness. He was confined to bed for close to two months.
The man had a wide circle of friends, a close family,
and an enviable reputation in the community. When
news of his illness spread, the hospital switchboard was
flooded with calls. There was barely enough space in
his room for either the visitors or the flowers. And the
mail poured in.

After a week, however, the crowds of visitors
thinned as people resumed their busy lives. There were
no more floral bouquets. Mail came almost to a halt.

The man had one friend, though, who went back
many years. This friend sent a small get-well card
when the man got sick. There was nothing special
about the card; it was far from elaborate. He sent
another card the next day, and then another. A get-
well card for every day the man was in the hospital.
Fifty-eight in all.

Once again, the message came through loud and
clear. This was no fair-weather friendship. This was a
friendship as steadfast as the stars.

18   Don't Be a Pitiable Case

We realize that in the last few sections, we've asked you to try things that may be difficult. In your present situation, the resulting strain may be overwhelming. So if you feel a need to weep and temporarily to break down, do it. At a time like this, it's essential to have some release. Feel free to go to pieces, but only in front of your therapist, parents, or friends—*not* in front of your mate. Don't give your spouse the chance to see you as pitiful, pathetic, unable to carry on alone.

If you instinctively feel that begging and hysterical sobbing will inspire nothing more than pity, you are probably right. Pity, of course, soon turns to distaste and then to loathing. Your mate may stick around for a few weeks to make sure that you don't kill yourself and then will flee at the first opportunity.

There's a second and more complex reason not to break down. You may think your spouse is leaving because he or she has found some special kind of strength, but the fact is that many people who walk out on relationships do so out of a sense of deep insecurity. Therefore, if you break down in front of your spouse, you may not only provoke her contempt, but you may very well trigger her own powerfully repressed feelings of despair and inadequacy. This will cause panic. *I always knew that a nobody like me could never get anyone*

*but a loser. Oh, God, look at him, weeping for me to take
him back. I better get out of here fast.* Here pitiableness
may be contagious.

We have told you in past chapters how important it is
to declare your love openly and unashamedly, to tell
your spouse at every opportunity that you love him or
her. Note carefully, though, that there is a world of
difference between saying, "I love you," and saying, "I
can't live without you." The former implies strength
and self-confidence, the latter merely self-absorption
and neediness.

At a time of marital crisis, it is more important than
ever to be strong and magnanimous. And if that's too
much to expect (and it often is), you must at least *act*
strong and magnanimous, even if you feel you are
falling apart. Your spouse can't read your mind, and
your inner feelings will not be nearly so obvious as you
think.

If you have a sense of humor, try to retain as much
of it as you can. Even on the battlefield, a funny line
can relieve a great deal of tension and foreboding.
Whatever you do, don't act as if you're feeling desperate. Few people are attracted to weakness; almost no
one to utter desperation.

Do Something Important for Yourself

It is essential to your mental and physical well-being
that you have "play," treats, something to look forward
to while you are working hard at rescuing your marriage. Make sure that you have a weekly tennis game, a
massage, lunch with a friend. Take time out to play
poker, to see a ball game, to work out at the gym. It is
not only a matter of pampering yourself but also a
concrete demonstration of your competence, your independence, your strong sense of self-constructiveness.

We realize, of course, that at times you may feel too
depressed to want to do anything or too panicked to
leave your home base for very long for fear that your
spouse will somehow disappear while you're gone.

Despite your fears, however, we recommend that you inform your wife that you are taking next weekend off to go fishing with the guys, that you tell your husband that you and a few friends will be attending an out-of-town conference on the arts.

Or what about starting roller disco lessons, tennis lessons, a night course in French, woodworking, yoga, or even massage? Sometimes one of the most pleasant outgrowths of such a pursuit is that you actually begin to enjoy what you are doing, learn a new skill, meet friends, discover new talents, develop a greater sense of self-worth. And when this happens, you may very well find that you are doing anywhere from a little to a whole lot less obsessing about whether your mate still loves you or not, whether he or she is going to leave you or not. And what a relief that can be!

Thus, if you sense that you have been suffocating your mate with your closeness, that he or she is becoming contemptuous of your dependency, maybe it's time to begin looking for a hobby or form of entertainment that is strictly "your own thing," something you like to do *away* from your mate. Imagine the surprise and even the vague jealousy he or she will feel at your sudden ability, even enthusiasm, to go blithely off for a few hours or days at a time—all by yourself.

Dress and Look Better

Now is the time to make a major effort to improve your wardrobe, figure, hairstyle. Physical attractiveness can go a long way toward making your mate feel better about you (and you about yourself). And the process of going to work on your appearance and figure can be fun, a pleasant change from the grim, difficult job of dismantling your mate's silence. We have previously pointed out the curious phenomenon that self-improvement campaigns are commonly undertaken after divorce, yet rarely beforehand.

We understand, of course, that beauty is only skin deep. Yet we would maintain that as simple a change as an improvement in your physical appearance could please your mate no end—to the point, in fact, where he or she no longer wants to leave you but instead wants to be with you, look at you, touch you.

Let us consider an example. Frank was growing increasingly morose around the house, snapping at the children for the slightest infraction, jumping up from the table as soon as dinner was through to sit in front of the TV set with the crossword puzzle. He rarely attempted to make love to his wife, Nancy, something that up until several months ago seemed to have been one of his fondest pursuits in their marriage.

Why was Frank acting in such a manner? It is difficult to say exactly. Perhaps it was the knowledge that he would soon be turning forty; perhaps it was a sense of frustration with his career (he had always dreamed of running his own company, and here he was after fifteen years still working for the same large paper manufacturer he'd started with upon graduation from business school); or perhaps it was just a cyclical depression, a temporary downturn in his spirits. Too often we assume that for every change in emotion there is a corresponding event, very precise and defined, which set it off. Books like Gail Sheehy's *Passages* and Daniel J. Levinson's *The Seasons of a Man's Life* have helped to correct this notion. Still, in many people, the feeling persists, and they assume that all periods of pessimism or elation or anger can be traced to a particular incident, such as a raise at work, a traffic jam on the way home from the country, a bad night's sleep, a flirtation with a co-worker at the office.

The conclusion that Nancy leapt to was that her husband had grown dissatisfied with her and was merely biding his time until he could figure out a diplomatic way to tell her he wanted a divorce. Having always had a tendency to *nosh* when nervous, Nancy began eating almost constantly between meals and soon was putting on a pound a week. Before long, her mildly plump figure was bordering on fatness. This seemed to exacerbate Frank's coldness, his aloofness.

Lovemaking between the two became ever rarer, occurring not even once a month, and when it did, always with Nancy as the initiator. Their relationship developed a vicious-cycle quality to it, with Frank's silent moroseness triggering increasing nervousness in Nancy, causing her to eat more, and her resultant weight gain causing him to withdraw further and further into himself.

Perhaps another couple might have been able to change the pattern through verbal confrontation, but that had never been Frank's nor Nancy's style. And so the problem continued, with Nancy getting heavier and heavier.

Oddly, it was Nancy's mother who finally intervened in such a way as to bring some relief to the situation. A frank, opinionated woman, she often stopped in to give advice on anything from childrearing to interior decorating. Possibly, it was her mother's strong, domineering personality that made it so difficult for Nancy to open any meaningful discussions with Frank, so used had she become as a child to keeping her opinions to herself. No matter; one morning, as Nancy was bustling about the kitchen making tea and toast, her mother, seated at the table across the room, declared, "You're getting fat, Nancy. It looks awful. You better do something about it. I'm sure Frank isn't very pleased."

Nancy, of course, had been harboring the very same thoughts, but hearing them spoken aloud, particularly from someone from whom she'd grown accustomed to taking orders, was enough to snap her into action. She began dieting and enrolled in an exercise program at a nearby health club. Within two weeks she'd lost five pounds, and her overly flabby arms and thighs had firmed up a trifle.

These immediate results pleased her immensely (even though she doubted that Frank had yet noticed the improvement in her appearance) and provided enough positive feedback for her to throw herself ever more diligently into her beauty program. She further reduced her intake of calories, upped the number of times she attended the health club, sat out in the sun, walked, bicycled, and did two sets of sit-ups a day.

Not only was the program therapeutic from the standpoint of aesthetics, but it helped to lighten her mood or, at least, to keep her mind off Frank's indifference. Suddenly, she had a purpose, a goal: to become impeccably trim. Each new pound lost, each half-inch pared from her waistline, buoyed her spirits, redoubled her dedication to avoid binging. Within eight weeks, she had reduced her weight to what it had been when she and Frank were first married. She retrieved some of her old sexy outfits from the attic, garments she had stashed away because she'd simply grown too stout for them. Before she got into bed at night, she walked about the bedroom naked, suddenly freed from the feelings of shame she'd experienced over her expanded belly and rear end.

Ultimately, his wife's improved figure caught Frank's attention. One night, soon after she climbed into bed and turned off the light, he slid over to her and wrapped his arm about her now slim waist. Before long they were making love, the first time he'd initiated the act in many weeks. The next morning, as Nancy moved about the room getting dressed, Frank seemed to be watching her from the bed. "You look pretty," he said. "Skinny."

Nancy exulted in his words. It had been a long time since he'd addressed her with anything near a compliment. From there on in, their relationship was marked by an unmistakable escalation of warmth and affection. Frank began to converse with her again, to look at her, to touch her, and Nancy responded with alacrity, for this was what she had been waiting for. Neither of them were really the type to talk about their inner feelings, but deep discussions were not necessary. The cycle had been broken, and they were able to return to their former level of friendliness, casual conversation, reasonably frequent lovemaking. Compared to where they had been, this was a vast improvement.

Now there are those who will ask how can we be sure that it was only Nancy's trimming down and firming up that was so instrumental in bringing Frank back into their marriage. We can't be. Probably there were other factors at play. Perhaps Frank, without even realizing it consciously, had resolved his conflicting feelings about his career and was once again ready to get on with the business of work and family. Perhaps, and this is even more likely, he'd simply arrived at the end of a cyclical period of depression at the very same time Nancy's appearance was improving and would have been set to embark on a happy upswing whether or not his wife had lost weight. Well, no harm done there. Certainly one would hardly aver that Nancy's conditioning program was a waste of time. At the very least, it had taken her mind off her present plight and had kept her from doing anything overly rash in reaction to Frank's moroseness. Too often, we, the authors, see husbands and wives move toward affairs, separation, and even divorce because a passing angry or depressive phase is seen by a spouse as a new and permanent stage in the marriage.

Ideally, of course, Nancy should have made some kind of attempt to dismantle Frank's silence. It is our opinion that the most permanent and complete reconciliations result when husbands and wives are able to talk about what they're feeling. But failing that, perhaps the best alternative for riding out a period of strain is a goal or pursuit that so occupies you that you cease to be obsessed with your silent, hostile, uncommunicative mate.

Nancy, for example, had she nothing else to keep her from dwelling on her marital problems, might have let her imagination run wild and assumed the worst. She might have sued for separation in an attempt to beat Frank to the punch, or tried to find a lover in order to repay Frank for imagined indiscretions, or smothered Frank with her company for fear of letting him out of her sight. Any of these desperate maneuvers would have exacerbated an already tense situation. Fortunately, though, Nancy put the marriage on hold and concentrated instead on doing something to benefit herself. In short, she remained off to the side, out of Frank's way, until the storm clouds that were haunting him blew away. And so even if it was not her fine new figure that lifted Frank's spirits but simply the passage of time, no damage had been done, no false conclusion leapt to.

You must keep in mind that feelings of positiveness and negativeness toward your mate will ebb and flow, heat up and cool down. Those persons who are mature and loving instinctively realize this. Unfortunately, millions of others, the divorcing public, do not. The first sign of rejection is often seen as the beginning of the end. Nonsense. The next day may bring hugs and kisses. And, of course, the day after that, coolness and hostility again. So what? We recommend that you remain calm and collected in the sudden face of new and unexpected hostility. The chances are it will not last.

We know from scores of interviews and case histories what a major influence physical attractiveness or the lack of it can have on a marriage. One young woman reports: "I began falling in love with my husband again the spring he started jogging. For the past seven years he'd been getting flabbier and softer. I actually found myself looking around at other men, contemplating an affair. And I didn't even feel particularly guilty. I've always worked very hard at looking my best, and I figured Albert owed the same consideration to me. In a way, I took his letting himself go as a personal affront. Was I supposed to look forward to getting into bed at night with a man whose belly had grown soft and huge? We were only in our twenties then, and sex played an important part in our marriage. Perhaps Albert sensed my disaffection, because I noticed him hovering nearer than ever at parties and dances. Then one day he came home with a pair of track shorts and jogging shoes. That alone made me feel more loving toward him. And, then, when he started losing all the weight and getting thin and handsome again, why, I couldn't keep my hands off him.

"I would agree that most middle-class women probably value a good wage-earner over a great-looking hunk who can't support a family. But when a man lets his appearance slip too much, it fills a woman with rage. If she doesn't work, it makes her feel so trapped. It's like, *Well, she won't leave me, so why bother to work hard at looking good?* It's inconsiderate when a man gives up on his looks. It's like saying, 'This is it, baby. What you see is what you get.'"

Think how much easier it is to like, feel affectionate toward, and forgive your mate when he or she looks particularly good as opposed to when he or she is having an "ugly day." It may not be fair, but it is, nevertheless, human nature. Quite naturally, many of us don't like to think that looks can play such an important role in a relationship that is supposed to be "holy" matrimony. Life shouldn't be so superficial. This book, however, is not about what *should* be; it is about what *is*.

Patchwork Solutions

Let us pause for a moment to reflect on a concern that may very well have come to mind. How can a blip upward in a spouse's physical appearance be anything more than a patchwork solution to something as problematic as a troubled marriage? Won't the underlying dissatisfactions rear their ugly heads once again when cosmetic solutions wear off?

Well, perhaps mastering a new skill or losing twenty pounds is indeed a patchwork solution. Perhaps many, even most, of the solutions in this book are patchwork, short-lived. But, then, maybe that's all they can be. The romantic notion of marriage as nonstop love affair is quite at odds with reality. Forget about those marriages that fail. You just have to run through your list of friends who have *remained* married to conclude that

rather than doting love matches, most of these unions
—even the very good ones—are characterized by alter-
nating phases of affection and hostility.

And what ends the bouts of hostility? What helps to
get a relationship back onto a smoother, more harmonious track? Why, usually, nothing more than little
things, patchwork solutions. She buys him a tie or a
cigar or a funny card while she's out shopping for
herself. He brings her a new blouse or a bottle of
perfume for no apparent reason. She, inexplicably,
feels like making love as they get into bed one ordinary
Tuesday night. He finds something she says over breakfast funny, and laughs. They are invited to a party by a
couple whose friendship they've been seeking and feel
proud of each other.

Lest we get carried away with only the positive side
of little things meaning a lot, let us not forget that
happenings of no more consequence than those cited
above can also unleash periods of bitterness and rage
between husband and wife: He walks around in his
blue blazer, oblivious to the dandruff collecting on his
shoulders; she looks drawn and plain when compared
to the wife of the couple with whom they are having
dinner; she gets a bigger Christmas bonus than he
does; he doesn't like his birthday present.

The point of all this is to underline the fact that
marriage is a living, breathing, constantly changing
relationship; and even when basically healthy and
positive, it is still marked by almost as much friction as
harmony. The notion that a solution to a marital
problem must be profound or lasting to be of merit is
naïve. Without too much of a stretch of the imagination, we can liken the course of a marriage to the
course of a life. There will always be little (and sometimes big) breakdowns: arthritis in the knee, pneumonia, heartburn, a fractured leg. These ailments can be
tolerated and often repaired. But it is fanciful, wishful
thinking that the human organism can be "fixed"
permanently, made perfect by "getting to the root of the
problem." Tomorrow or the next day a new difficulty

will crop up, and except in the rarest of cases, this is the way it will always be with human bodies and marriages. The sooner we all accept this, the easier it is to get on with the business of our lives and the less we will be defeated by the realization that most cures are not cure-alls but more likely simply repairs, stop-gap and patchwork in nature.

This is why we, the authors, feel so strongly about the potential of revitalizing one's interests or improving one's physical appearance. True, it might not work every time or even for a very long time. But you only have to think of how elated you can feel at the sight of your mate coming downstairs looking well dressed and trim and more attractive than usual to understand what a powerful instrument of reconciliation this can be. And unlike more amorphous and philosophical solutions, such as changing careers or starting psychotherapy, looking better is something that is tangible, real, and often achievable in just a few days. It may not work forever, but it does work.

Amaze Your Mate

We're going to ask you to try to accomplish yet another thing that may at present feel as if it is beyond you. Amaze your mate. Perhaps your spouse has decided you are a pitiful wretch who cannot survive on your own. Hah! Take a trip with the children or, even better, without them. Go to a tennis camp, skiing, a dude ranch, on a bicycle trip, to Club Med. Begin venturing out at night, to lectures, movies, plays. Take dancing lessons.

If you're a full-time homemaker, get a job or at least a part-time one. Even the most ordinary of jobs can stimulate you, give you a sense of independence and optimism. We cannot stress the importance of this enough. It is astonishing how much self-esteem an occupation can impart to those who have not held a job for years. And, of course, there is nothing like office or store or factory life to make you feel you are part of a family, part of a group of people who are your friends.

There are many other ways to amaze your mate. Change jobs to one that is obviously much better or more interesting than the one you had. Take up a musical instrument or resume playing one that you were proficient at in your youth. Start a novel or ballet lessons or a cooking course, even a small business at home. Go back to college to complete your degree. Do things that take you away from your mate, both emotionally and physically, so that he or she wonders what you are up to.

This may also be the time to give in to any heretofore unexpressed urges to flirt, to be festive and lively when you and your mate are in a group. A little healthy jealousy can be immensely effective in making you look vastly more attractive to a mate whose interest has been flagging.

Our experience has been that people who think that they are in the process of losing a mate often suppress impulses and avoid opportunities to interact with members of the opposite sex for fear that it will push their already disaffected spouse over the edge, out the door. Generally speaking, almost nothing could be further from the truth. If your mate is beginning to find you less and less attractive, often all he or she needs to see is someone else flirting with you, dancing with you, desiring you, to experience a sudden renewal of interest. This kind of reaction is what disinterested husbands and wives suddenly feel when they are informed that their mate is taking off, without them, to attend a teachers' conference for the week: *Oh, my God, my mate can exist without me. I better inject myself back into his or her life.*

Our only caution here is that you not overdo it. The arena of flirtation is an explosive one; and while provoking mild amounts of constructive jealousy in your mate is often an excellent way to renew his or her feelings of love and desire for you, too much jealousy can lead to psychotic behavior. Be particularly cautious if past experience has indicated that your mate has a history of pathological jealousy or a potential for overreacting and violence.

Demonstrate Your Superior Qualities

In his need to build a case to leave, your mate has probably been concentrating on your idiosyncrasies and weaknesses, and turning a blind eye to your finer qualities. Don't let him. Even more important, don't let him convince you that you've got nothing to offer.

You must consciously work to remind yourself of your superior qualities. Write them down ahead of time. And just as you do when preparing a résumé, list *everything* that's good about yourself. You may want to ask a friend to help you make sure you haven't left anything out. (We are often our own worst critics.) This accomplished, tell your mate as fully as you can just what a superior person you are. Make him or her nervous about what he or she might be giving up: "You'll never find anyone who'll spend as much time with the kids as I," or "You're going to miss my back rubs more than you think." Do this often ... and about everything.

A mate who has declared his or her intention to leave may be vastly more conflicted than you suspect. The slightest new shred of input can sometimes be enough to change his or her mind, make your mate decide to stay instead of taking off for the unknown.

Imagine, for example, that your wife is leaving dull, stolid old you for a man who, on the surface anyway, appears to be far more impulsive and artistic, romantic and devil-may-care. Do not suppose that it hasn't occurred to her that the very same character who extemporaneously bolts out of the car to pick daisies for her hair may also be the type who is less than meticulous about more mundane things, such as earning a living or helping your kids with their homework. If your son in Little League belts a homer because of a slight adjustment you've made in his batting stance, don't think it too trivial to communicate this to your wife. It reflects well upon you and may just give her pause. *Hmm,* she might think, *Porforio is far too caught up in the new play he's writing to spend time with little Barry. I don't think he knows a baseball from a playbill.*

We want you to understand, of course, that we are not implying that reminding your mate of your good points will automatically bring her back to the fold. But in talking to those people who have been deserted or who are in the process of being left, we have found that many describe a feeling of helplessness, of wanting to do something but not having any idea what will be effective. Continually reiterating for your mate your achievements, your talents, your outstanding qualities, is as good a place to begin as any. Not only will it give you a sense of purpose, but it's powerful advertising.

Of course, even more important than *telling* your mate of your superior qualities is to *demonstrate* them. If you've been postponing a pursuit at which you excel or have the potential to excel because you've been too depressed or absorbed by the problems of your marriage, we recommend that you throw yourself back into your hobby or career with a vengeance. Success makes believers—nay, even worshippers—out of almost all of us.

We know of one case, for example, in which a man won back his wife simply by doubling his salary. Joan and Ted had bickered for over a decade, often about money. Joan dreamed of a bigger house, finer furniture, more expensive clothes, and constantly upbraided her husband for not having the wherewithal to indulge her. Joan's enthusiasm never failed to sting Ted to the quick, for he loved her deeply and always felt vaguely inadequate and guilty for not being more of a success. One day, Joan announced she was leaving and, with her two young sons, moved out of the modest house she shared with Ted to return home to her parents.

For a while, Ted was immobilized. But having more time on his hands than he'd had for years and desperate to take action of some kind, he brought his portfolio of direct-mail letters to another advertising agency, where he was immediately offered a job at twice his present salary. He was stunned. Looking for a better job was something he had contemplated for the past three years, yet the problems of his marriage had been paralyzing him. Everything seemed too hopeless, too difficult, too much work.

Joan's response when Ted phoned her about his new job was euphoric. She returned with the boys the very next day, as happy for her husband and his restored sense of self-esteem as she was for herself. The additional money did not cure all their problems, but it certainly alleviated a lot of the backbiting and bickering.

We are certain that there are those of you who might fault Joan for her fair-weather sailing, her shameless ambition, her materialism. And, indeed, perhaps she should be faulted. But as we pointed out earlier, this is not a book about morality, about what "should be," but rather one based on sound principles of human behavior. This is a practical, actionable manual offering advice, we hope, that you can use to rebuild your marriage.

Remember, the nobility and selflessness and romanticism that characterizes certain husbands and wives in literature are found in short supply in living, breathing human beings. There are many more Joans in real life than Juliets, and it is pointless to maintain that Ted should not have taken Joan back because she was obviously interested only in his money. Since when are money or looks or social status unimportant? A marriage is not dissimilar to a business deal. Two parties are drawn together because each possesses something that the other one wants. Perhaps your husband chose you because you come from a socially prominent family. Maybe your wife was attracted to you because of your great build. If you allow these assets to lose value—by not making contact with your prominent friends, by neglecting your physique—then you will lose leverage with your mate. You'll now have *less* of what he or she married you for.

In a mature relationship, of course, people find new qualities to value in their mate. But how many relationships are all that mature? And would *you* want to stick around if your spouse suddenly put on fifty pounds or lost his or her source of income? On the other hand, isn't it that much easier to feel good about your wife when she comes back from the office and tells you she got a $5,000 Christmas bonus, or your husband wins a Betamax for leading his department in sales? It is natural to be drawn to a winner.

Thus, if you are a teacher who has always dreamed of starting your own nursery school or a good amateur saxophonist who feels you can earn a second income by starting a band, now may be the perfect time to do what you have to do to excel. Now may be the time to sublimate for the moment your concerns about your marriage in order to fulfill your promise. By doing so, we maintain, you may very well be increasing your leverage and thus your appeal to the man or woman you fear you are losing. If you have superior qualities or skills or talents, don't hold back. Demonstrate them for all the world, particularly for your disaffected mate, to see.

19   Professional Help

Practically everyone needs some kind of help during the crisis of a crumbling marriage. Most of us will initially turn to our families or our closest friends, our co-workers, the family doctor, or our pastor. Informal advice and guidance, especially if it is sound, is often all we need. Sometimes, though, it is wise to seek more professional help.

There are few decisions more difficult than choosing the right therapist, especially when you are going to need his or her help in solving the problems of two people: you and your spouse. Just because you are willing to pay top fee or just because the doctor has diplomas stretching from wall to wall doesn't mean that he is the right person for you or that the therapy he will provide is going to help your marriage. It might, or it might just be the last nail in the coffin.

If you decide on professional help, then, how do you find the right professional? "Psychiatrists, social workers, psychologists, psychoanalysts—it's so confusing," you may say. "I only want to find someone who can help save our marriage, not help do it in."

You can't forget the horror story your neighbor Raymond told you last month. He and Margie were having their problems, and Margie said she wanted to see a psychiatrist "to get her head straight." Raymond thought that this might be just the thing to get them back on the right track. He agreed and sent the doctor a check every month, patiently waiting for things to get better.

After a month or two of therapy, Margie moved out of the bedroom. Now she's stopped talking to Raymond at all—on doctor's orders, she claims. It will interfere with therapy, she says. She's trying to reach her full human potential. Translated into English, that means that she's thinking of walking out. On doctor's orders.

The point of this story is not to avoid professional help but to be awfully careful in selecting the right helper. The trick is to find a therapist who has the skills and motivation to hold a marriage together. If your spouse decides to get help first, then you must do everything in your power to ensure that he or she sees a real therapist, not a marriage wrecker with a degree.

Family Therapy

It is best to find a therapist who will see the two of you together. You must resist the temptation to go into individual treatment with the hope, probably, that you will find someone to agree with you and help you tear down *in absentia* that so-and-so who has had the gall to split.

You must then persuade your spouse to accept a therapist who will see the two of you together. Few husbands or wives, no matter how eager they are to leave, can flatly refuse a request to "give it one last chance," if only for the welfare of the children. This is not guilt-induction. It is reality, for the welfare of the entire family is indeed at stake.

Whether the professional calls himself or herself a marriage counselor, a couples therapist, a pastoral counselor, or a family therapist is not of primary importance. These are just labels. What is significant is that he or she is willing to see both of you and to continue to see both of you. Sometimes he might speak to you alone and sometimes to your spouse alone; but sooner or later, he will sit you both down in the same room, insist that you talk together, and begin working directly on your marriage.

If you and your spouse can find such a professional, there is an excellent chance that he will help; at the very least, he will not make your marriage worse. A therapist who believes in *seeing* both partners together is one who generally believes in *keeping* both partners together.

That man or woman knows that there are two sides to every story, that no one is ever all right or all wrong in a relationship as complex as marriage. He won't sit idly by while the wife wallows in self-pity about all that her husband has done to poor little her; or while the husband describes the demure woman sitting next to him as a demanding bitch. He will point out that it usually takes two to tango and help you recognize how each of you has been contributing to the problem, perhaps how you are triggering each other off.

A therapist who understands relationships knows that people don't stay together for one or ten or twenty-five years out of the goodness of their hearts. He will not accept your spouse's claim that the marriage "has never been any good," for he knows that there must have been a lot good about it for the two of you to have come together in the first place and to have stayed together for any length of time. He will let both of you vent your outrage and your hurt, then help you explore the issues, gain perspective, and put the pieces back together. He will help your husband rediscover why he once fell head over heels in love with you, or your wife acknowledge that she once thought you were the only man in the world. Then, working forward, he will help the two of you find out what went wrong.

Does this all sound too simple to be true? Well, that's just how it works. The problem is that many psychiatrists have a lot of rigid but dearly held theories about what makes people tick. Many believe that anything short of private, individual therapy is second-rate.

They look down their noses at the prospect of seeing a couple together.

"That's not real therapy," they'll sneer. "That's marriage counseling."

Translated, this means: "The hell with your marriage. I'll practice what I get a kick out of practicing."

Let us tell you about a colleague—a psychiatrist—who, almost by accident, ended up doing the right thing for his patient before it was too late. Evan, a forty-five-year-old druggist, consulted Dr. A. because he was depressed. He had decided for himself that he was depressed because of his wife.

Evan and the doctor met for an hour each week, and the man's description of his poor mate was embellished with each telling. Dr. A. had to admit that despite a valiant attempt to remain neutral, he subtly got caught up in his patient's vivid tales. *Selfish. Uncaring. Insensitive. A lazy spendthrift. What a royal pain!* he found himself thinking. *Boy, if I were married to that lady, I'd be on my way to the nearest lawyer.*

Now, psychiatrists usually don't come right out and tell their patients to get divorced. They pretend to be impartial, but it's very difficult to be impartial when you hear just one side of the story, week after week. Dr. A. tried to be nonjudgmental and nondirective. By his sympathetic listening, though, he was abetting his patient in his view of things and probably adding a little fuel to the fire.

After several months, Evan wasn't getting any better, though he had pretty much decided to pack his bags. Dr. A. didn't know what else to do, so, in desperation, he suggested that his patient's wife, Irene, join them for a session.

Evan turned ashen. "She'll never come," he almost screamed. "Haven't you been listening to me? She doesn't give a damn!" But he agreed to ask her anyway.

The lady didn't take much inviting. She couldn't

believe that she had been asked. She didn't trust Dr. A. very much at first. Being excluded from the sessions, she had always envisioned her husband and his therapist as two old buddies at the men's club shooting the bull about women in general and herself in particular.

This time Dr. A. played his cards right. He didn't take sides but simply sat back and let the couple talk. Once they got started, they couldn't stop. They said things to each other that they hadn't said in years. Angry things, but also tender, loving things. The doctor had plenty of time to observe, but he did not anticipate what would unfold before his eyes.

No question that Irene was hurt and upset. Beyond this, though, any resemblance between the wife sitting in the consulting room and the witch that her husband had described was purely coincidental. Irene was beautiful. She was sensitive. She was bright and obviously caring. Her husband's eyes opened wide in amazement as he began to see his wife again, for the first time in many years.

Now, isn't that screwy! Why should two basically normal people pay a doctor just to be able to *talk* to each other? Maybe it is screwy, but we'll tell you something that's a lot worse: two people paying two doctors to *keep* them from talking to each other!

This case had a happy ending. Evan and Irene stayed together. Evan discovered that his wife was not the cause of his depression, but that his job of counting pills in the drugstore was. He felt that he couldn't do much about his dissatisfaction at work, so without even knowing it, he displaced all of his frustrations onto his spouse—an understandable enough human reaction but one that could have spelled tragedy.

Individual Therapy

What if you can't find a doctor who sees couples? (When we use the word "doctor" we are not referring to a man's or woman's academic credentials and are not necessarily talking about a psychiatrist or psychologist. We know many professional men and women without doctorate degrees—from such fields as social work, education, nursing, or the clergy—who are superb therapists.) Let's now consider a few general rules for choosing an individual therapist, if individual therapy is the way you must go.

While labels can be misleading, we strongly urge you to avoid anyone who calls himself a "psychoanalyst," unless he convincingly assures you that he will attempt to *help* you, not to psychoanalyze you. Orthodox psychoanalysts (those are the silent ones who ask you to lie on the couch rather than sit up and want you to come at least three times a week) are notorious for undermining their patients' marriages, if not by design then by neglect. Even healthy marriages do not often survive traditional psychoanalysis. This is an emergency. You need the doctor's expertise to help you come through a crisis in a troubled relationship, not to delve leisurely into the intriguing mysteries of your childhood fantasies.

Whether it is you or your mate who is considering an individual therapist, make sure you know with whom you are dealing. There are some therapists whose patients all seem to get divorced, and others whose patients seem to stay married. This dramatic difference in outcome is due in some part to the doctor: to his training, his theoretical bias, his skill, his attitudes, and even to his own marital situation.

While you have no real way of evaluating these complex factors, you can at least check the therapist's reputation in the community. Is he a marriage doctor or a divorce doctor? Ask his former patients. If all else fails, ask him directly: "Doctor, in the troubled marriages that you have seen in your practice, tell me candidly, what's your track record?"

Regardless of the therapist's official qualifications, it is essential that you have a good feeling about him or her. Trust your own initial impressions. Is this a person you can like and respect? Is he easy to talk to? Does he seem sympathetic to your plight? Or does he sit staring at you with all the emotional display of a professional poker player?

Like any other doctor, a psychiatrist has an obligation to discuss your condition with you—his diagnosis, his prognosis, and his treatment plan—and to obtain your informed and knowing consent as to what he plans to do. Avoid any mental health professional who refuses to tell you what he thinks is going on, or who deflects your legitimate questions about his proposed therapy with questions of his own. If you get bad "vibes" from the first visit, pay your bill but do not come back for a second—find someone else.

If Your Spouse Insists on His or Her Own Therapist

This spells danger and calls for you to be more involved and active than ever. Under no circumstances should you simply agree, wishfully thinking that it's bound to do some good. You would be deluding yourself if you assumed that any reasonable doctor will see how ridiculous your mate is and knock some sense into his or her head. The doctor is going to know only what your less than unbiased spouse feeds him—unless, that is, you have been able to have some input.

It is tricky enough to choose your own individual therapist; it takes even more tact and judgment to influence your husband's or wife's choice. Do not stay out of it, though, in the hope of appearing noble or of not provoking your spouse's rage. It is essential that he or she find someone who can help. There are too many professional marriage destroyers in the phone book for you to sit back blithely and let your mate choose one.

Let's say your wife is the one who is unhappy with the marriage, and her best friend has recommended Dr. X. Your wife needs not only your support but your help paying the doctor's bills. You've got a foot in the door.

"Maybe Dr. X. will help, but first I want to meet him

or at least speak to him" must be your first approach. If your wife refuses, forget it, for this therapy probably won't work. If the doctor refuses, then really forget it.

Would you want your wife to see an internist who adamantly refuses to talk to you about her heart condition? A psychiatrist is a doctor, not a CIA operative. Certain things need to be kept confidential, but be wary of any therapist who makes too big an issue about confidentiality. That therapist probably doesn't understand much about the way marriages operate and almost certainly underestimates the importance of open communication when people have stopped talking to each other.

Let's say everybody agrees and you meet your spouse's therapist. Three things will happen: You'll be evaluating him; he'll be evaluating you; and you'll be stating your best case for the marriage.

You want to convey to the doctor in no uncertain terms that you are willing to do what has to be done to make this marriage work. Let him know how much you and your spouse have invested in the relationship. Bring your kids to the office to meet him and then leave them in the waiting room. The therapist won't miss the point that there's more than one life involved. He'll see that this is no make-believe family, and he'll think twice when your spouse asks his advice about separating.

Needless to say, dress your best and look your best. Remember three strategies: Be reasonable; be reasonable; and then be ever more reasonable. Let your spouse rant and rave. That won't do anyone any harm. Stay calm.

But it's not just you trying to make a good impression on the therapist. If he expects you to support this enterprise, he's got to make a good impression on you. Put him to the acid test by asking a few simple questions.

"Doctor, do you believe in keeping couples together?" is as straightforward as any. If he answers with a simple yes or, at least, "I try to, if at all possible," you might have found the right helper. If he waffles, if he says, "Yes, but . . . ," and then goes on to tell you about good divorces and bad divorces, or about people needing to find themselves first and worry about their families later, forget it!

"Doctor, may I call you if things are not going well at home?" If he answers, "Sure," then fine. If he starts to make a speech about the sanctity of the doctor-patient relationship and his vows of confidentiality, tell him it was nice knowing him. You didn't ask him to divulge your spouse's secrets. All you asked was if you could call for help if your married life began to fall apart.

These maneuvers may seem intrusive, but they are usually readily accepted by both the estranged spouse and the therapist. Generally speaking, if your husband or wife does not invite you to participate in his or her therapy, it is not for the purpose of excluding you. Odds are that your mate thinks that you do not care enough or that you are too angry to put yourself out, and fears a blistering rejection of any invitation he or she might offer.

The doctor would probably like to meet you, too, but he has little choice other than to accept his patient's word that you will not RSVP. Most responsible therapists, including individual therapists, actively welcome the opportunity to meet significant figures in their patients' lives. It makes doing therapy a whole lot easier.

Sex Therapy

Less than two decades ago, a pair of researchers named Masters and Johnson revolutionized the understanding and treatment of human sexual problems. Prior to the publication of their pioneering work (*Human Sexual Response*, 1966), sexual dysfunctions were generally assumed to be the direct result of either deep-seated emotional problems or of bad marriages.

Common sexual difficulties—impotence or premature ejaculation in men, or inhibited orgasm in women (a condition that used to go by the chilling name of frigidity)—were conceived of as mere symptoms of some more underlying condition. One had to treat the underlying condition to cure the symptom, just as one must treat the pneumonia if the cough is to go away.

If a married person sought help for a sexual concern, he or she was doubly damned. The very existence of the problem was seen as proof positive that the individual or the marriage was deeply flawed.

It now turns out that many people with sexual dysfunctions or sexual incompatibilities are physically and psychologically healthy in every other way. The specific problem is often the result of rather immediate causes, such as sexual ignorance, self-consciousness, or performance anxiety.

Sex-therapy techniques are not designed to make people over. Rather, they focus on limited and specific goals, and are concerned purely with the improvement of sexual interaction. Therapy is brief and direct, and both partners are involved. Specific sexual exercises, compatible with the couple's social and religious values, are prescribed for the man and the woman to do at home together. Office sessions are used to discuss the partners' progress and to make suggestions for improvement. More extensive marital issues are avoided. Success is measured by the disappearance of the presenting sexual symptoms.

We have discussed the rationale for sex therapy at some length to make one essential point. *You and your spouse may be having marital problems because you are having sexual difficulties, and not the other way around.* In that case, the treatment should be aimed at the sexual difficulties, and not at the marriage.

If you and your mate have had a satisfying sexual relationship until your third child was born, or until you both lost your jobs, or until Mother came to live with you; if the disorder has come on rather suddenly, perhaps after a serious illness; if the two of you are having problems in bed but are perfectly compatible in every other way, chances are that you would benefit more from sex therapy than from psychiatric treatment. In the absence of more extensive emotional turmoil, the prognosis for complete recovery is usually excellent, particularly if the problems are not allowed to become chronic.

We are quite aware that many married people (particularly men) tend to panic when their sexual prowess is threatened. While a man may be disgruntled at his wife's unresponsiveness, he will become a basket case if he himself cannot perform, and may bolt in panic.

The remedy to your sexual difficulties may be a lot less painful than you realize—it might even be fun—and you must reassure your spouse of this fact before it is too late. It would be tragic if your marriage foundered on what is now an eminently treatable condition.

Treatment of Alcoholism

One of the most common yet unrecognized causes of marital turmoil is alcoholism. Chronic alcoholism has been called the hidden disease. If someone is seen shooting heroin, even once, he is instantly branded a drug addict. It is difficult, on the other hand, to draw the line between normal drinking and problem drinking, since it is often a matter of degree. It may take years or decades for the family to recognize that Dad or Mom, a model citizen in every other way, has become an alcoholic.

Alcoholism has also been called the disease of denial because the alcoholic will not admit even to himself that he can no longer control his drinking. A couple of car wrecks this year? Anyone can have an accident. Came to work tipsy? Just a little unexpected celebration. Spit up some blood? Must be the ulcer acting up again.

It is unusual for an alcoholic to walk out of a marriage; it is generally the spouse who leaves when he or she can no longer tolerate the endless lies, the accidents, the economic losses, and the social embarrassments. He or she may walk out because of one

drunken argument too many, or because the children
are now grown, or because he or she is just too weary
to put up with it any more.

If your spouse has threatened to end the marriage
because of your drinking, it is *you* who must take
action. Are you really an alcoholic? Ask your friends
(not your drinking buddies) for an honest opinion. Tell
them that you really need to know. Ask your family
doctor or your pastor or your boss, and be prepared to
accept the truth. Don't get hung up in semantics.
"Problem drinker," "heavy drinker," and "borderline
alcoholic" are generally euphemisms for the same
thing. Alcoholism is a treatable disease, but only if you
are willing to abandon your denial and recognize that
you need help. Our experience has been that the spouse
will usually stick around if the alcoholic acknowledges
that he or she has a problem and goes about doing
something to solve it.

There are many treatments for alcoholism, and different ones work best for different individuals. Some
treatments involve psychotherapy and others the use of
medication or behavior modification techniques. Your
family doctor should be able to point you in the right
direction, or at least refer you to a mental health
professional for a consultation.

The single most useful treatment for most people is
Alcoholics Anonymous, and the AA approach has
probably helped more drinkers than every other therapy combined. AA is an international self-help organization with groups in practically every city and town in
the United States. The local groups are not run by
professionals, but rather by recovering alcoholics
themselves. Members come from every ethnic, racial,
and socioeconomic group, and from every walk of life.
Most groups are open to all comers. Some are special-
ized, such as Physicians' AA, Lawyers' AA, even
Priests' AA. Auxiliary organizations such as Al-Anon
are designed for the non-drinking spouses of AA members and are effective in helping the couple work on the
problem together in a constructive way.

Nonprofessional Help

During these trying times of working at winning back a mate, it is important to have allies, friends, people who you feel are on your side. Whether or not you seek professional help, most of you will naturally turn to your friends for advice and support, and that is good.

Some people cannot bring themselves to speak to anyone, so strong is their need for privacy. These are the folks who keep everything to themselves, who put on a strong front for the outside world while their inner world collapses. When their marriages fail, their friends invariably react with shock: *Impossible! They were always such a perfect couple!*

It is a mistake to keep all your pain under lock and key. Friends are warm and comforting, and will listen to your rage and grief and despair and let you cry on their shoulders. This is good. This is what they are there for. Use them to let out your pain, your secret fears. Let them cheer you up and coddle you. If they are good friends, they will be only too happy to serve such a function. To a lonely, cornered person in the midst of a marital crisis, friends are essential, life-sustaining. Don't be afraid to turn to them.

But friends can confuse. Without realizing it, they may misguide you as a result of their own unconscious feelings of jealousy or hatred toward you. Or perhaps they are working out fantasies of their own. Your pal urges you to let go of your straying wife because he'd really like to get rid of his own. Your divorced neighbor counsels you to leave your cruel and loveless husband because she wants someone else to hang out with on Friday and Saturday nights, or perhaps she wants to see if she can land your husband herself.

Whether you and your spouse remain together or eventually break up is something you—and only you—can decide. Ask your best friend, the one who is telling you you're better off without such a thoughtless and manipulative mate, how he or she would like to spend

New Year's Eve alone. It's very easy to dispense with someone else's mate, particularly when you've got your own all safely tucked away at home. Remind your "friend" that for every person who "finds" himself or herself through divorce, three to four probably drown.

The fantasy seems to go something like this: Okay, you've been left. No loss. He or she was a destructive, inhibiting force. Now it's time to pick up the pieces, start analysis, begin jogging, make yourself perfect. This accomplished, the next step is to set out to find a new and perfect mate, someone attractive and sensitive and kind and possibly even rich.

We will admit that all of the above are both possible and even admirable pursuits. But let us consider the reality, which is far grimmer and more limiting, for the truth is, most people *don't* change; *don't* suddenly get wiser; *don't* stop making the same mistake; *don't* cease being attracted to lovers who are "wrong" for them; *don't* find new resources of energy, creativity, intelligence; *don't* start living life to the fullest. Instead, they plod on in much the same manner as before, albeit now alone, now without the imperfect but nevertheless present companion of several or many years' standing. The reality is, sadly, that divorce is more likely to change you for the worse, not the better.

Another complication to be avoided when involving friends or relatives in your marital woes is to resist the temptation to let them fight your battles for you. If they want to set you up with a wonderful blind date and you're willing and able to participate, fine. But if they want to call your mate on the phone and give him or her a piece of their mind on your behalf, don't allow it. It is too easy for your mate to stand up to your friends and relatives, much more difficult for him or her to be confronted by you. To use others is an indication that you feel too weak, frail, unworthy, or that you don't really care enough to take action yourself.

20   Lawyers

Sandy was at the end of her rope. Her husband, Neil, had not been home in three days. She knew their marriage had been bad for at least a year, but never had it been this bad. She was certain Neil was having an affair. Even if he wasn't, this latest episode of irresponsibility was too much.

Sandy called her mother. "Mom, what do you think?"

"I told you that you should never have married him. He's worse than your father was. If I were you, I'd divorce him and never let him see the kids again."

"Thanks, Mom," Sandy said weepingly, then dialed her best friend. "Lisa, what should I do?"

"Do!" Lisa exploded through the phone. "Get rid of the bastard. Change the locks and call the police if he tries to get in. Hang up if he calls."

"I'm just not sure," Sandy replied. "I just don't know."

"Look, Sandy, nobody likes to think about ending a marriage, what with the kids and all. But I did it, and I survived. Why don't you talk to my lawyer? He did a good job for me."

Neil didn't return that night, so Sandy called Mr. M. first thing the next morning. She was a little taken aback when he told her he would see her right away.

M.'s office looked like a Hollywood set: plush green carpeting, mahogany furniture, and a wall full of photographs of the lawyer shaking hands with politicians and movie stars. Sandy had been waiting only a few minutes when M. walked in.

"Thank you for seeing me so quickly. Lisa L. sent me. I'm having some marital problems," Sandy said softly.

"What kind of problems?" M. asked, not unkindly.

"My husband, Neil, and I have been fighting for at least a year. I think he's seeing someone else. He hasn't been home in four days."

"Four days!" the lawyer exclaimed. "Tell me, what does your husband do?"

"He's a college professor."

"Too bad," the lawyer responded. "Teachers don't earn all that much. But they are reliable and they can't hide their income. Before you leave, I want you to fill out this form listing your husband's salary, his assets, any property that you and he own. Don't forget anything, no matter how trivial, or else we won't get it."

M. glanced at his Patek Philippe watch. "It's almost eleven-thirty. The banks close at three. I want you to go down to your bank and empty out all your savings and checking accounts. Then go home and look for any bonds or stock certificates—in fact, any valuables you can find: coin collections, jewelry, and so forth. Take a large vault at a bank that doesn't know you, and stick it all in there. Use a different name. But you've got to do it before he suspects anything."

Sally's heart was pounding and her head felt light. "But I'm not sure. Is all this really necessary?"

The lawyer smiled and leaned back in his large leather chair. "My dear young woman, no one is ever sure. It's my job to protect you. If you change your mind, you can always give it all back."

"If you say so," Sally whispered.

"Beg pardon. I didn't hear you."

Sally cleared her throat. "If you say so."

"Good. Do you have any children?"

"Two," Sally replied. "Jessica is eight and Paul is five."

The lawyer smiled and lit a cigar. "Fine. He's not to see the kids until we get him to agree to a temporary settlement. I'll start drafting the papers, and we'll serve him in the morning . . . if we can find him, that is. After you've done your bank business, I want you to call my secretary and give her a list of all the things he's done to you, all the reasons he's an unfit father and so forth."

"Unfit father!" Sally felt a bit stronger. "Neil is wonderful with the children."

"I'm sure," the lawyer retorted. "That's why he's been gone four days. Look, the point is not to deprive him of his kids, but believe me, he's going to have to start paying if he expects to see them again. Don't worry. I've been in this business twenty-five years. Leave everything to me."

Does this seem like a bizarre scene from a Grade B detective movie? In a way, it is. But it happens all the time. The courtroom scene in *Kramer vs. Kramer* is tame compared to most.

Lawyers are nice people, but we have a so-called adversary legal system in this country, and that system isn't always so nice. Lawyers are supposed to be advocates for their clients and do everything in their power (short of being unethical) to fight for their clients' interests, at least their short-term interests.

The adversary system usually works quite well when a lawyer is suing your landlord, or fighting an unfair summons, or defending you against a criminal charge. It breaks down, however, in domestic disputes, because the litigants continue to have to deal with each other through every stage of the tortuous divorce process and for many years beyond. Unfortunately, the adversarial process encourages people to act out their most vengeful instincts, and divorce attorneys not infrequently fuel the aggression. If the spouses are angry before litigation, they are usually irreconcilable after it.

Lawyers

195

Sally consulted an attorney because she was confused and hurt. At the stage she saw Mr. M., she needed a counselor, not an advocate. M. only inflamed his client's passions and unnecessarily escalated the conflict.

It is not a lawyer's job to initiate a reconciliation, and one should not seek a lawyer's help for this purpose. Before taking legal action, however, M. should have helped Sally explore what she really wanted and told her what she could reasonably expect. And he should have insisted that she consider her options and forbear from acting hastily. We sometimes liken consulting a divorce lawyer to bringing your car to the car wash: Once your bumper is hooked up to the chain, there's not much you can do to derail the process.

We understand that a lawyer is not a psychotherapist, and it would be inappropriate for him to probe the depths of his clients' emotions. On the other hand, an attorney can create untold hardship if he plays upon his clients' fears and provokes a marital war. Whoever drops the first bomb can be certain that the other side will soon retaliate in force. And when the bombs start dropping, the fallout will pollute the entire family.

A small band of progressive attorneys and mental health practitioners have begun a movement called divorce mediation. While these divorce mediators do not see themselves as attempting to salvage marriages, they try hard to prevent their clients from behaving destructively or vengefully. The lawyers become sophisticated in methods of therapy or at least work in tandem with qualified therapists. They are not very popular among the established divorce bar, but they seem to be making progress.

Joseph L. Steinberg, a Connecticut marital lawyer and an articulate spokesperson for divorce mediation, cautions attorneys about taking their clients' requests at face value, particularly in the initial interview. In an article in the *American Bar Association Journal* (May 1976), Mr. Steinberg points out that " 'I want a divorce' is a universal cry with a myriad of meanings." Some clients, of course, really want a divorce. Others are simply conveying that they are scared or angry or hurt. Some want to be able to strike the first blow. Others do not want to end the marriage but would like to secure their financial position, just in case.

In the article, Steinberg implies that a lawyer is not required to start litigation the moment a new client steps through the doorway. "A therapeutically inclined attorney recognizes the latent ambiguity and listens for clues to the reluctance that lies just beneath the surface. A substantial percentage of potential divorce clients are truly eager to have their reluctance exposed and their uncertainty clarified."

This book is about staying together, not getting divorced. If you are having marital problems, though, you can be sure that you will feel the urge at some point to seek legal counsel. In your anger, you may even be tempted to make some sort of preemptive strike. Once you hurl the first grenade, though, it cannot be taken back. So be cautious.

Avoid divorce attorneys unless there is absolutely no choice, because they usually make matters worse. Lawyers like to fight—they are trained to fight—and they can be very expensive. They often have few qualms about asking for huge retainers, which not infrequently offset any financial advantages you may gain.

If your spouse is threatening to leave, attempt to arrive at an interim pact. "If you don't retain an attorney, I won't either. Even if we can't save our marriage, let's work out the issues face to face. It will save us both a lot of aggravation and expense. If we absolutely cannot agree, we can always call in the lawyers later on."

It is a fact of life that lawyers are sometimes necessary to defend your real interests, particularly when it becomes apparent that your marriage will not last. If you decide you need to see a divorce attorney, we advise you to use as much caution in selecting one as in choosing a therapist. You may well need his or her protection at some point, but, in Joseph Steinberg's words, you should seek "a healer as well as a warrior."

Check out the lawyer's reputation in the community. Do the divorces he handles turn into bloodbaths? Can her clients and their ex-spouses talk to each other? Can they live with the final verdicts or are they constantly back in court seeking justice? Has he any training in family therapy or mediation, or does he view such things as a waste of time? Ask him directly: "Have any of your clients ever reconciled?"

Stay away from any lawyer who advises you to communicate to your spouse only through her. Avoid a lawyer who becomes too enthusiastic about your cause and treats your divorce as if it were her own. Shun a lawyer who fills your head with unrealistic expectations, couched in such phrases as "We'll take him to the cleaners," or "She won't get a red cent."

Do not empty bank accounts, kidnap the children, hide your spouse's possessions, rip up the credit cards, or swear to false or misleading statements. Most of you would not commit kidnapping, perjury, or theft in dealing with a stranger; you shouldn't do it with a spouse. Listen to a lawyer who advises you to act like a gangster . . . just long enough to report him to the ethics committee of the local bar.

Never use the children as pawns. If you are genuinely worried about the way your spouse treats the kids, then you must take appropriate action. But don't let a lawyer blow a minor incident between your spouse and your kid into a case of child abuse. If the children ask for intimate details of your marital problems, tell them to mind their own business. You don't need the protection of a kiddie brigade.

A lawyer does not have to be bloodthirsty to be effective. Whatever the short-term advantages of adversarial combat, they are certain to be canceled by the resulting vindictiveness and lust for revenge. Potentially salvageable marriages are not infrequently permanently destroyed by the fighting that takes place after the decision to separate.

We have heard many divorced husbands and wives say, "I might have tried to make a go of it but not after what they did to me in the divorce negotiations." If you and your attorney succeed in cutting off your spouse's legs, there's no way he or she will ever walk back.

21   Recoupling

All right, nothing in the previous sections has worked. Your mate has moved out. Or perhaps he or she has forced you to move out, literally had you evicted by a judge's decree. Is it time to give up? Only if you've decided you no longer want your departed mate. If that's not the case, there are still strong reasons to continue to believe that you will ultimately prevail.

You may be assuming that your husband is holed up in a love nest with his new paramour, that your wife is going to the opera every night with a lover in tails. The reverse may be true. Your mate is now without you and without all the tenderness and support and care that you gave him or her over the past years. Your spouse will be feeling a void, a sense of loss and grief, even if he or she cannot admit it.

So it is important when you do speak to or see each other for you to be as warm and supportive as your mate remembers. This can have an immensely powerful effect in triggering all those latent feelings of love and genuine affection that he or she furiously repressed in order to get over the hump of leaving you. To be cold now would be to keep your mate away, but to be warm and accepting could be just the thing to bring him or her back.

See Your Mate Whenever Possible

If your mate wants to see the children (and they live with you), or come by to check on the tropical fish tank, make it easy for him or her to do so. Now is not the time to be petty or difficult. And be there when your mate arrives. Use this chance to talk, to be friendly, to be comforting. Your conversation should consist of (1) how well you are doing and (2) blithely stated, your endless desire to have him or her back.

About the latter suggestion we anticipate a concern. *"Won't I seem pathetic to keep asking my mate to come back? Won't I appear the very picture of the spurned lover?"*

Our answer is that you *are* a spurned lover. Your mate has left you. What is so bad about that? Surely at least half the people of the world have been losers in love once in their lives. There is a stigma to the role only if you let it overwhelm you. Being spurned is not pathetic. What is pathetic is going down without a fight, pretending that you don't care, not speaking up for what you really want.

We see nothing demeaning in your saying to your husband, who has come to take the kids for a visit to the zoo, "Gee, you look great, Harry. I sure would like to have you back."

Even if at the time he has no intention of returning, you've delivered a message that is unmistakably clear. You want him back. If tomorrow he wakes up in his tiny, overpriced studio apartment, a hangover burgeoning in his brain from having drunk too many stingers the night before while he prowled the singles bars, unsuccessful in his search for a young easy score, he may recall your words: *"I want you back."* Yesterday they seemed pointless and uninteresting. In the gray light of this depressing Monday morning, they might be resonating with an inviting warmth. Who knows? Perhaps he'll pick up the phone and ask you to meet him in town for lunch. And if he does, accept.

Let us reemphasize that you should see your estranged mate as often as you can. Keep the lines of communication open, but keep them free of anger and recrimination. Your mate does not want to return to the gloomy, pessimistic atmosphere from which he or she has just exited. An atmosphere of depression can remain in your estranged mate's mind for days. That is why there should be an upbeat aura to you and your home. He or she will not be drawn back to a funereal picture of despair.

On the other hand, if you look reasonably happy and independent, as if you've adjusted rather well to your new life as a single, your mate might think twice. *Aha, Edna is a far more self-reliant person than I thought. What have I given up?*

To continue our scenario, you and your estranged husband have met for lunch. Say it again: "I meant what I said yesterday, Harry. The kids and I would love to have you back."

Here, tone is all. Try not to sound weepy or pathetic, as if you will go to pieces if he does not oblige. Nor should you sound stern, as if he has been a bad boy. He does not want to return to a feast—yours—of recriminations. He does not want to be married to a schoolmarm. So simply state the fact, pleasantly, affectionately, and with dignity, that you love him, you want him back, he is still the main man in your life. The key word is "magnanimous." You are not spiteful or desperate. You will not die if he does not return. You will just enjoy life so much more if he does.

If your estranged mate requests to see you, accept. Or if you feel an impulse to see him or her, don't stand on ceremony. Give your spouse a call. "Let's have lunch," or "Come over for dinner," or "I've got an extra ticket to the tennis matches," or "Wendy asked that you come over and take a bicycle ride with her."

Whatever your excuse, try to see your mate as often as you can. And when you do, never fail to state your desire, calmly and matter-of-factly, that you sure would like to have him or her back.

Furthermore, do not refuse drunken, sentimental, or late-night requests for rendezvous. When people are separated, these requests occur with astonishing frequency, particularly when the leaver phones the person he or she left. Why?

Perhaps your wife's new career isn't turning out to be as glamorous as she had fantasized. The job she was promised as assistant buyer is starting to feel strangely like that of glorified secretary. She feels that she's been had and needs to see you for some of your wonderful old-fashioned warmth. Definitely agree to meet her. Now is the perfect time to ask her to come back.

Married people who leave often find that life out there is a lot rougher than they had anticipated. At some level they begin to question whether they haven't made a mistake. They can rarely admit their doubts to themselves, and almost never express them to their spouse. At best, they can drop hints and hope that their spouse will pick them up.

So if your husband calls you from the corner pub having had one beer too many, don't slam down the phone in a rage. The common response is to think he is lording his new freedom over you. That would be a gross misinterpretation. He's reaching out to you in the only way he can without destroying his dignity, without admitting his need. Take the hint. If you want him back, don't turn him away. Difficult though it may be for you to believe, his call is an overture. Take him up on it.

Look Good

Easier said than done, but make an effort to look your best whenever you see your mate. If you look attractive, your spouse will carry this image around in his or her mind for the next several days, wondering if perhaps he or she hadn't made a terrible mistake by leaving you.

One man told us that he left his wife in the early

stages of their marriage for a colleague whom he considered to be much more attractive. His wife panicked. She lost her appetite and almost immediately thereafter dropped fifteen pounds. In an attempt to attract a new lover as quickly as possible, she outfitted her new svelte frame with a smashing wardrobe. As it turned out, she attracted an old lover.

About a month after he had left, her husband was taking the bus home from work. He glanced out the window and his eye was caught by a slender pretty woman in a red dress, who, upon closer inspection, turned out to be his wife. There was a sad, soulful cast to her eyes, and she looked quite beautiful to him, so much slimmer than he remembered. *What am I doing,* he thought, *heading home to someone else when my own wife is just as pretty, and I love her so much more?* He called her that night, and they were together again for keeps the very next week.

We stressed the importance of looks in an earlier section of the book. And we do it again. Because looking good, although it is certainly not the most important thing in the world, can still be enormously persuasive in winning back a love.

Drop Your Mate a Note

Phone or write your mate often to declare that you love him or her, that it would make so much sense to get together again. If you are rebuffed, don't go to pieces. Be supremely confident. Simply say, "That's okay. I'm here. I love you. I've met others, but no one compares to you. And why should I settle for anything but the best?"

A woman from the Midwest reports that after she and her husband separated, they sold their house in order to divide the proceeds. When she was finally settled in a new apartment, she sent him a simple note informing him of her new address and phone number. He telephoned that very evening, claiming that just the sight of her handwriting had nearly moved him to tears. He had forgotten how neat and precise it was, the obvious pride she had always taken in its style and perfection. The image of her sitting at her desk, forming her letters with concentration as she bit her lower lip, popped into mind, and he felt an overwhelming desire to see her, to be with her. And, thus, his phone call, all because his wife had dropped him a few lines in the mail.

The couple began dating again and shortly after resumed living together. They report that although they still quarrel a lot, they remain married, and their relationship is basically working.

Do Not Be Lured into Bed

On those occasions when you are spending time with your estranged love, being warm and accepting as we suggested, you may feel an urge to hop into bed. Try not to. If you do succumb, however, make it clear that you are doing it because you enjoy it, not because you want to please. Don't let your spouse thank you; you're not doing anyone a favor but yourself.

Be mysterious. Once in bed, do new things, things you might have learned from someone else. Don't get weepy and sentimental. Don't become clingy. Otherwise, sooner or later, your mate's old, familiar feelings of antagonism will return. You are still pathetic. You have submitted.

On the other hand, if you resist, you may be aiding your cause in ways you never even imagined. Who says your estranged mate is having a rich and plentiful sex life away from you? How can you be sure it's better and in fact not a hundred times worse? More than a few of the deserting husbands and wives we interviewed spoke of missing, unexpectedly, the physical intimacy they had shared with the mate they'd left.

Naomi's story is not atypical. "I missed his aroma,"

she said. "Whenever I spent the night with a new man I would lie there remembering how it was with Ken. What I liked best was cuddling together in the morning. His smell was delicious to me, suffusing the room, lingering on the sheets. Sometimes I would feel a mad urge to call him up just so I could come over and sleep with him.

"But after the first few times, whenever we did get together, he would refuse me. He said it destroyed him for weeks afterward. His resistance is what brought me back. I swear to you, no one else was like him, no one else made me feel as comfortable in bed, as if this was where I really belonged. I think that more than anything is why I came back to Ken."

Date, If Possible

During this period of separation, it is important to date. You will automatically throw off less desperate "vibes." Whether you sleep with your dates or not is up to you. You should be aware, however, that even though you are the one who has been deserted, a jealous wife or husband can return to commit suicide, murder, you name it. You've got to be sane and sensitive in this area, particularly when you consider the legal ramifications a love affair can have on any divorce settlement.

On the other hand, constructive jealousy can work wonders. Often, nothing brings a mate back faster than the realization that his or her magical "hold" on reliable old you is no longer working.

One man reports that he could not return to his wife fast enough when he learned she had moved into her own apartment. The two had been living with their baby daughter in a small rented house in the suburbs of a large southern metropolis. When the husband split, his wife returned to her parents' home with her child and remained there for several months while she tried to put her life back in order. Once she felt strong enough, she took a job and a small apartment in town.

As soon as he heard that his wife had moved into her own place, the husband called for a date. The two saw each other several nights a week for about a month, going out as if they had recently met. "But I couldn't take it," said the man. "My wife is a reasonably attractive woman who has always liked men and sex. I knew it would be only a matter of time before she was going to bed with other guys on the nights when we weren't together. Sure I was playing around. But that's me. I couldn't bear the idea of her doing the same.

"One night I called to take her to the movies, but she said she couldn't, she was busy. She didn't say doing what. I almost went berserk. I called and called and called, until around two in the morning she finally answered. That was it. I rushed right over, and we've been back together ever since.

"I've never been able to worm out of her whether or not she was sleeping with anyone else. Sometimes it still torments me, a dozen years later. If I didn't have that fear, I'm not sure I would have ever come back. I was having too good a time."

Go out anyway even if you don't feel like it. Attend concerts, movies, lectures, shows, dances, massage courses, yoga courses, anything. Activity gets you out of yourself and gives you a sense of community with others, replacing your desperate dependence on your estranged mate.

You may even meet someone to date. This often happens when you least expect it but is not likely to happen if you sit home in front of the TV set. So go out often, even when you're not in the mood.

You never can tell when magic is going to strike.

The major impediment to recoupling is a belief that it can't happen. Yet it happens all the time.

In America today, there are millions of husbands

and wives who separated and who are now back together. Some even go so far as to divorce and then remarry . . . each other.

The point is that reconciliation is eminently possible if you don't hide behind false dignity, if you don't let pride and rage get in the way.

22   Epilogue

An experienced divorce lawyer we know of put the issue this way:

"You know, I don't think people try hard enough. At the first sign of any real trouble, they assume the marriage is dead, and they come in to ask me to help them bury it.

"If they are the ones being left, they seem too embarrassed to ask their spouses not to go. They often give up without much of a fight, and if they do fight, it's about the divorce settlement.

"In many years of practice, I've seen it over and over again. One couple in a group of friends gets a divorce, and then the others go. It's a real domino effect. Why don't more of them stand up and say: 'Hey, I'm not going to let this happen to me!'?"

No one seems to have had much success understanding our national divorce epidemic, and we have no such pretensions. In this book, we have simply tried to speak to those husbands and wives who are threatened with being left, and to tell them that it doesn't have to happen. Just because a marriage is ill, the prognosis doesn't have to be fatal.

We recognize that some marriages should never have seen the light of day, and the sooner laid to rest, the better. We hope that no one will interpret anything we have said as encouraging a battered wife to attempt to win back her sadistic husband and have him abuse her some more.

Divorce is at times a necessary evil; however, it should not be exalted as some kind of liberating adventure. Your spouse may be convinced that leaving you is a stage of maturity, something like breaking away from his or her parents. Nothing could be further from the truth. You have got to realize this, and you have got to make your spouse realize this as well.

We live in a cynical age. In the frantic search for fulfillment, it seems, it's everyone for himself or herself. Whatever the merits of this underlying philosophy, it is consummately short-sighted if it leads to a belief in marital dissolution as cure-all. If your spouse walks out, he or she will soon enough come face to face with the sobering fact that it is not you who is at the root of all his or her problems. It is quite unlikely that simply leaving you will bring your mate the happiness and self-fulfillment he or she expects. Once again, you have got to realize this, and you have got to make your husband or wife realize this, too.

In some circles we have seen the phenomena of divorce announcements, divorce parties, and even divorce rings—all rather desperate attempts at pretending that a time of sadness is really one of joy. There is no joy in ending a relationship, either to the leaver or to the one being left, and certainly not to the other members of the family. As one patient rather succinctly put it after receiving her final decree: "You know, when you get divorced, it's not like when you get married. There's no one there to celebrate."

For those of you who have decided to take a stand, we have tried to dispel the unwarranted hopelessness that is often the lot of the person being left. We can all understand the agony of losing a lover and feeling powerless to do anything about it. But marriage is not just any love relationship. Your mate married you for what seemed like good reasons at the time; he or she has a lot more invested in you than you may believe;

and he or she is more ambivalent than you might imagine.

You are, in a word, not trying to win back a stranger but rather your husband or wife. And therein lies your leverage. In this book we have tried to show you how this leverage can be effectively used.

We have given many case examples and have made numerous suggestions that have done the job for others in your situation. There is nothing tricky or under-handed about any of the approaches we have set out. You need not mark your copy of this book "Top Secret." If your spouse wants to read it, fine. If nothing else, it will disabuse him or her of any notion that you don't care.

Much of the popular self-help literature suggests that before you can accomplish whatever it is you are setting out to do, you must first learn to love yourself. Nonsense. You can't *learn* to love yourself. Feelings of self-esteem can come and go, ebb and flow, seem to be cyclical in nature.

The fact is that you can continue to function, contin-ue to pursue the goal of repairing your relationship, even when your feelings about yourself are less than glowing. You must simply continue to put one foot after the other. As you do, your mood will brighten, and you will eventually begin to see results. Many a great accomplishment has been achieved by people who were at their lowest.

Be wary of movements that promise to restore self-love. During times of diminished self-esteem, we often cast about wildly for something, anything, to make us feel better about ourselves. Be careful. Throwing your-self into some bizarre group that promises to foster self-love by having you chant strange imprecations can take your eye off the ball. You don't want to join a monastery of religious cultists. You want to win your wife or husband back. Concentrate on that instead.

The threat of marital separation is a crisis, not a tragedy. It represents a time for action, not for mourn-ing. If you are not paralyzed by fear or rage or stubbornness, chances are you can turn this crisis into an opportunity for growth. Some people have the odd notion that once wounded, a marriage can never be whole again. Actually, there are countless couples who, having come through divorce crises, ended up with marriages stronger than before.

There may be times when, assailed by self-doubt, you are ready to lie down and be sacrificed. Don't. Accept your feelings of despair, but keep plugging away. Life is fickle and complex; changes for the better occur when you least expect them. Internally you may feel resigned to a failed marriage, but do not under any circumstances hang your head and tell your mate it is okay for him or her to go. The danger is you will do this just when he or she is ready to turn around and give the marriage another try.

There are too many cases of an estranged mate suddenly returning just as it appeared that he or she was involved with someone new. Do not give up prematurely. Continue to tell your mate, "I am here, and I want you back." Often that simplest of declarations is enough to start him or her thinking about how nice it would be to be back home.

So keep hope. And fight on, even if you're hardly in the mood. It's not your mood that counts. It's your actions that will dictate your success.

ABOUT THE AUTHOR

ERIC WEBER is the author of many best-selling books, including the world-famous *How to Pick Up Girls*. President of a publishing firm, he is also a novelist, screenwriter, and film director. He lives in Tenafly, New Jersey, with his wife and four children.

STEVEN S. SIMRING, M.D., is a clinical associate professor at the New Jersey Medical School in Newark and a practicing psychotherapist. A diplomate of the American Board of Psychiatry and Neurology, he lives in Englewood, New Jersey, with his wife and two children.

SPECIAL
MONEY SAVING
OFFER

Now you can have an up-to-date listing of Bantam's hundreds of titles plus take advantage of our unique and exciting bonus book offer. A special offer which gives you the opportunity to purchase a Bantam book for only 50¢. Here's how!

By ordering any five books at the regular price per order, you can also choose any other single book listed (up to a $4.95 value) for just 50¢. Some restrictions do apply, but for further details why not send for Bantam's listing of titles today!

Just send us your name and address plus 50¢ to defray the postage and handling costs.

BANTAM BOOKS, INC.
Dept. FC, 414 East Golf Road, Des Plaines, Ill 60016

Mr./Mrs./Miss/Ms. _____
(please print)

Address _____

City_____ State_____ Zip_____

FC—3/84